A Different Kind of Man
Changing Male Roles in Today's World

Richard P. Olson

Judson Press ® Valley Forge

Library of Congress Cataloging-in-Publication Data
Olson, Richard P.
  A different kind of man : changing male roles in today's world / Richard P. Olson.
    p. cm.
Includes bibliographical references.
ISBN 0-8170-1263-X (pbk. : alk. paper)
1. Men—United States. 2. Men—United States—Religious life. 3. Men's movement—United States. 4. Masculinity—United States. 5. Masculinity—Religious aspects—Christianity. 6. Sex role—United States. I. Title.
HQ1090.3.057 1998
305.31—dc21   97-52186

Printed in the U.S.A.

10 09 08 07 06 05 04 03 02 01 00 99 98

5 4 3 2 1

Contents

"In the growing field of books for Christian men, *A Different Kind of Man* is long overdue. Judson Press has given us a great tool for understanding the situation of Christian men and boys and their spiritual needs. Dick Olson revisits his 1982 book, *Changing Male Roles in Today's World*, with a cornucopia of new material. Olson is precise and accurate in his insights. His holistic approach to the needs of Christian men will be a tool for mature discipleship—and men need tools!

A Different Kind of Man is more a ministry than a book. It is rooted in understanding the manhood of Christ and will take new life in the heart and daily walk of any man who reads it."

—Dr. Z Allen Abbott
Executive Director, American Baptist Men, U.S.A.

Acknowledgments

I am grateful to the men who read, reviewed, and offered suggestions chapter by chapter. These included Bill Pate, Gary Peterson, Scott Stannard, Dr. Z. Allen Abbott, Dr. Joe Leonard, and Dr. Bob Southard.

I also express my appreciation to Terry Chaffee, B.S.N., for her informed and helpful suggestions on chapter 3, "Feelings." I am thankful to Bev Cosby for her very efficient and able efforts in helping to get this manuscript in its final form.

I am also grateful to members of the editorial staff at Judson Press: Kristy Pullen, Mary Nicol, and Victoria McGoey. Thanks to each of them for their part in this effort.

1

Is There a
Men's Movement?

It was an innocent question, but it gave me a chuckle.

I had been given two copies of the same book as Christmas presents. And so I took one copy to a local branch of a national bookstore chain and asked the manager if I could exchange it for something else. Since I had just begun the investigation that would lead to this book, I asked if the store had a section on the men's movement. It didn't. I inquired where books on the men's movement could be found. The manager thought for a moment and then asked me, "Is this fact or fiction?"

Amused by the question, I turned away quickly so she would not see my grin. But then I stopped to think. Scanning the shelves, I did not find any books on the men's movement or men's issues that I had not already read.

I wound up selecting a book a friend had recommended, *Reviving Ophelia* by Mary Pipher.[1] Pipher gives us a sensitive and powerful examination of what a harsh culture is doing to the selves of adolescent girls. She tells the stories of those girls and of her attempts as a therapist to help them find power and heal. This book deeply touched me, and I longed for a counterpart volume about the effect of our culture on the selves of adolescent boys. Only much later did I find Michael Gurian's excellent book, *The Wonder of Boys*.[2] Advertised as speaking on behalf of boys as Pipher did on behalf of girls, Gurian's book is a start, but much more needs to be done.

As I reflected on what I did not find at the bookstore and the message of the book I did find, the manager's question came back to me. This time it was not so funny, but rather uncomfortable. Is the men's movement fact or fiction? It is not so clear, big, and bold an entity that it demands its own section in an average-size bookstore.

A Hurt, A Hunger

Clearly there is a pain and a hunger in many of us men. We want a movement, or at least more mutual support, and are ready for whatever will provide that support. The hunger extends over the generations and across the races of males. The pain takes many forms.

Some of us are lonely. We search for satisfying relationships with both men and women. We long for ways to belong that feel natural. This loneliness extends into our very families. Some of us feel an emptiness and pain with regard to our own fathers. At some important points in life, we did not receive what we needed. And we fear we don't know how to give what is needed to our sons and daughters.

Further, we see others (mostly women) who are so free with their emotions, who cry when tears are appropriate and who laugh with abandon. And we wonder why we feel so stuck and closed inside. We are so out of touch with feelings, so far from being able to express our emotions, even to feel them. Sometimes, when we do start to express our feelings, we are frightened at the rage and violence that erupts from within us.

We live in a tough, competitive workplace. We work hard just to stay even, and we fear we will not "get ahead"—whatever that means. But it's difficult to find anyone with whom we can share our fears. We wonder if it is weak or whiny for us to talk about the difficult issues that many of us face.

With our wives or potential lovers, we'd like to walk in a beautiful garden of intimacy, affection, sex. Instead we seem to wander in a wilderness in which the paths to closeness are overgrown or not existent. Little is clear. Yesterday's model of a husband is out of date. We would like to know how as a husband to build a good relationship.

We're sick of the humor that puts males down. We're weary of being blamed for most of the problems of society. And, for that matter, we're tired of being ashamed of being men.

Certainly there is something good, something dignified, something worthy in my maleness, but what is it? And what does it mean to be masculine, anyway? What do I need to do to be "man enough"? What do I need to be?

At the same time, we recognize problems in our society —homelessness, poverty, violence, gangs, children and youth adrift, racism, violence against women—for which all of us bear some responsibility. Leadership from revitalized men with inner strength could help build a sane society.

We'd like a spirituality, a walk with God that fits us. We may have depended on the women in our lives to "do the spiritual stuff" and to provide the spiritual energy. We know that isn't fair, and we want to relate to God for ourselves in our own unique ways. We long for that vital firsthand relationship with our Creator. We'd love to be empowered for ourselves, for others, for our world. But we're not clear how to do that.

Some Problems That Deserve Attention

Many assume that males, particularly white males, occupy places of privilege and power beyond what they deserve. I am one of those privileged white males, a middle-class, financially secure professional person. I enjoy safety, nutrition, health care, influence, and opportunities beyond what many in my land enjoy—and certainly far beyond what people in many parts of the world have available. There is another side, however. In certain areas men are at greater risk, suffer more, lose more, and so live with great problems. While this is true for all males, it is even more true for African American males, and true to a frightening degree for young adult African American males.

Warren Farrell was for many years a member of the board of directors of the National Organization for Women. Although he applauded the many insights and achievements of that organization, he gradually came to feel that some issues and injustices for men were being ignored. In *The Myth of Male Power,* he notes a number of places where men are in places of dis-privilege.[3] For example, speaking of the "death professions," he notes that 94 percent of all people killed in the workplace are men. Further, only men are required to register for the draft. Though we currently have an all-volunteer army, only men would be required to report for military duty if an emergency arose. In the twentieth century, over 99 percent of people killed in wars have been men. In the current armed forces, women in service have combat options, but only men have combat obligations.

And again, men commit suicide five times more often than women. Nearly 100 percent of all political assassinations have targeted men (granted, when more women are in leadership, they will be more liable to this attack). Over 99 percent of those executed are men. The street homeless are approximately 90 percent men.

In regard to disease, men die sooner than women from all of the ten most lethal diseases. And this leads Farrell to his most telling statistic of all. In 1920, men died only one year sooner than women. In the 1990s, men's life expectancy was seven to eight years shorter than that of women! Part of this change may be due to decreased deaths of women in childbirth, and we rejoice in that health gain for women. At the same time, however, we must ask what society is doing to us or what we are doing to ourselves that decreases our life span to that degree.

In response to these needs, interesting changes have been happening among men. Gifted, thoughtful men have offered a variety of analyses and a number of cures for these pains that are unique to males. A number of helpful leaders have arisen over the last few decades. And these leaders are finding ears ready to listen!

It probably is a fiction to talk about *a men's movement* but certainly not to talk about *men's movements*. Each movement touches a particular hurt or hope; each finds a response in the men whose need it touches. Over the last three decades, at least seven movements have arisen to respond to men's needs and hurts and offer support and leadership.

The 1970s: Learning from the Wisdom of Women

The first men's movement can be linked with the goals of the *profeminist movement*. In the early 1970s, the women's movement gained momentum. Although some men responded with a backlash to what the women desired, others identified with the women's agenda. They asked how they could support women's new discoveries and, further, whether some aspects of that older patriarchal society were harmful to them as well. Those males who fell in the latter category—who embraced these goals of women and longed for corresponding female wisdom in men—became part of the profeminist movement. Jack Balswick recalls, "Our goal was to create a new male, one that was more feminine than the macho one we had been raised to emulate."[4] Herb Goldberg's book *The New Male* provided a theme in its subtitle: *The Feminist Movement Can Save Your Life.*[5] This early men's movement was more effective in reaching men in academic circles than working-class men and was helpful in establishing men's studies programs on several campuses.

I am one who was attracted to this part of the movement. I grew up on the plains of western South Dakota, acutely aware that I did not fit the male stereotype of cowboy, rancher, tough guy. Rather, I was interested in relationships, intimacy, sharing feelings, helping folks through listening; I was fascinated by children; I felt the strong appeal of words and books. When I came upon a men's literature that claimed these "female" tendencies for males and worked for deep respect and equality between the genders, I was drawn to that point of view. My earlier book *Changing Male Roles in Today's World* was written from a male profeminist point of view.[6]

Much in this viewpoint still appeals to me. It invites men to pay attention to the full range of their experiences and emotions as men, to know all of themselves. Far from merely reacting to earlier movements, it invites men to be more fully human. At the same time, more remained to be said.

A second men's movement took shape in the seventies, the *gay-affirmative movement.* Persons in this movement affirmed that much could be learned from women, and indeed they were a part of the early men's movement described above. However, they added one concern. They would seek full acceptance of persons regardless of sexual orientation. Gay rights along with women's rights and minority causes were part of their agenda. Full acceptance of all people into society without fear, repression, or persecution was and is their compelling vision.

The 1980s: Discovering the Hidden Wisdom of Men

In the mid-1980s, a different kind of men's movement with new leaders and new spokesmen emerged. There had been some stirrings, meetings, writings earlier. However, when in 1989, Bill Moyers's interview on public television with Robert Bly, "A Gathering of Men," was broadcast, the movement burst upon the American scene like water released from a floodgate. Bly's *Iron John,* published in 1990, was the first book on men's issues to appear on the bestseller list, and it stayed there for thirty weeks.[7] In 1991, Sam Keen's *Fire in the Belly* also made it to the list of the top ten bestsellers.[8]

This was a distinctly different movement, not an outgrowth of the earlier one. A 1988 anthology of pieces from acknowledged leaders of the earlier men's movement did not include a single reference to the most influential thinkers in this newer movement: Joseph Campbell, Robert Bly, Robert Moore, or Douglas Gillette. Nor do these writers cite the writings of persons in the earlier men's movement.[9] The newer movement was characterized by one main thrust, the mythopoetic movement, and at least two other efforts connected to particular needs or causes.

Those in the *mythopoetic movement* seek the wisdom and experience of men of all cultures and ages. Their goal is to help men discover the unique aspects of their manhood and to initiate boys into manhood. Rather than calling men to develop only their feminine side, this movement encourages men to develop a full range of masculinity through a wide-ranging exploration of male spirituality and psychology. Using the insights of psychologist Carl Jung, men are introduced to ancient literature, poetry, art, dance, and ritual, including Native American traditions. They sense that perhaps myth, legend, fairytales, and poetry are transmitters of ancient and enduring truth about who men are and how they are to communicate wisdom to each other.

Mythopoetic leaders fear that in the modern industrial society something vital for men has been lost and must somehow be recovered. (I speak in more detail about what they believe to be essential maleness in the next chapter.) Men may find like-minded men and stimulation through small support groups, monthly councils, or several-day retreats in rustic settings.

The mythopoetic movement has captured a good deal of attention. Few are neutral about it. Some men believe that it connects them to an unnamed hunger, a longing they felt but did not recognize. Others see it as self-indulgent and filled with meaningless rituals, while it ignores the pressing problems of today's world. Others detect a rejection of women, which they find troubling. Whatever one thinks of it, this movement influences thinking and presents provocative questions to all who seek to understand themselves as men.

The *men's rights/fathers' rights movement* is a fairly small but committed and visible group. In this group are persons who realize the truth of Warren Farrell's conclusions in *The Myth of Male Power.* They recognize where males are in places of legal dis-privilege and abuse and lobby for changes where they see the need for men's rights. They are concerned with such matters as child custody, child-support awards, visitation privileges of divorced fathers, the rights of unmarried fathers. They also speak out against male bashing in the media and male-only draft laws.

The *addiction/recovery movement* is another distinct male movement. Found within the various twelve-step programs that began with Alcoholics Anonymous, this male movement has an additional agenda: confronting the grief that many men have over an unhappy relationship with a father figure.

Those drawn to this movement speak of such issues as "woundedness," "toxic masculinity," and the "inner child." Their goal is to heal from a hurtful past inflicted on them by males and to claim the strength to be a different kind of male for those whose lives they touch.[10] Father absence and father wounds are the central focus of this movement and may indeed be among the deepest needs that propel all of the men's movements.

The 1990s: Toward a Wider Vision and Spiritual Renewal

In recent years two powerful men's movements have burst on the scene. One arose in response to a Christian man's vision. The other was an expression of a population often not touched by the movements described above. Let us consider each in turn.

The largest wave in these men's movements is one of the newest and is distinctively Christian—the *Promise Keepers movement.* In 1990, Bill McCartney, then football coach at the University of Colorado, had a discussion with a friend about the need for discipleship in men. Out of this he developed a dream and a concept. He pictured Colorado's Folsom Stadium filled with men who had come to focus on Christ and their own spiritual growth. Such a large men's gathering was held and grew each year, until, in 1993, all 50,000 seats in Folsom Stadium were filled. It has since been held in other stadiums and has reached hundreds of thousands of men annually.

Journalist Verne Becker describes the Promise Keepers' stadium events:

> For only 55 bucks [now slightly more] including meals, you get a combination of church service, revival meeting and training seminar that stretches from 6:30 p.m. Friday to 10 p.m. Saturday. Nationally-known evangelical ministers and church leaders give the main addresses, and Christian recording artists lead the crowd in singing lively worship and praise songs. The atmosphere is serious but upbeat, and the focus is unabashedly evangelical in both teaching and fervor.[11]

Those who participate are urged to keep seven promises that the organization has identified as fundamental to a man's spiritual growth. Here, briefly, are the seven promises:

1. to honor Jesus Christ through . . . obedience to God's Word in the power of the Holy Spirit
2. to pursue vital relationships with a few other men
3. to practice spiritual, moral, ethical, and sexual purity
4. to build strong marriages and families
5. to support the mission of one's church
6. to reach beyond any racial and denominational barriers to demonstrate the power of biblical unity
7. to influence the world by being obedient to the Great Commandment (Mark 12:30-31) and the Great Commission (Matthew 28:19-20)[12]

The emphasis on promise keeping is seen as one of the many reasons for the widespread appeal of this movement. Many of the other movements have lent insight but not clear guidance concerning what to do with these new discoveries.

Men, mostly from evangelical or charismatic churches, gather to be led by the men who have a vision for them. Sports and military metaphors are widely used—as they are in the Bible. Songs, chants, and waves rock the stadium. Edward Gilbreath, writing in *Christianity Today*, recalls a moment at one of the events in Boulder:

> The men erupt in laughter as preacher Charles Swindoll, clad in faded denim, rides into the arena atop a Harley-Davidson motorcycle, the savage vocals and scratchy chords of "Born to be Wild" blaring in the background. Later in the evening, author and speaker Gary Smalley displays some wildness of his own, making his entrance on a kiddy-sized Big Wheel bike.
>
> "Promise Keepers is a fun thing as well as a serious time for men to grow," says Nate Adams. . . ."An important aspect of the conference is the chance men have to express their boyish and playful sides."[13]

Indeed, Gilbreath notes, many of the men he talked with were excited not so much by what was being said as by the opportunity to "hang out" with other men.

Inspired by the dynamic speakers, the power of being together, and the promises made, men return from the mass gatherings to their home communities. Men's accountability groups are developed in many communities to support men in their search to fulfill their commitments.

Promise Keepers is widely but not universally praised. Some observers believe that despite the ecumenism of the sixth promise, an underlying assumption of Promise Keepers is that only fundamentalists and charismatics are real Christians; critics also question the literalist interpretation of the Bible practiced by many of the movement's adherents. Further, women pastors are not encouraged to attend the ministers' events, and thus, some fear, the authority of women clergy is undermined. Others feel that Promise Keepers promotes a hostile attitude toward existing communities of faith because it points to a loyalty beyond existing denominations—possibly to a superchurch they will call into being. Still others fear that the movement confuses religious faith with nationalism and patriotism and that it points to a theocracy—a rule of the nation by the "laws" of the Bible rather than by constitutional democracy.

Of course everything has two sides. A friend of mine, a denominational leader of men and someone who has participated in a number of Promise Keepers' events, responded this way: "As a Christian member of a denomination I love, do I have the concerns of which you speak? Yes, I do. But I feel the power, the inspiration, the stirring up of men to a new commitment and responsibility, is much stronger than any reservations I have." As with every other movement, we will be wise to heed Paul's words in Romans 14:5, "Let all be fully convinced in their own minds."

Promise Keepers is the largest and most visible of the explicitly Christian men's movements. It is by no means, however, the only one. Rick Koepcke and E. James Wilder find at least six streams within the Christian men's movement. Some of these parallel the "secular" movements we have already described. They are concerned, respectively, with (1) men's liberation (with encouraging men to develop their own "feminine qualities"); (2) coaching, or discipling, models, of which Promise Keepers is the prime example; (3) healing, particularly from the father wound; (4) fathering; (5) male sexuality (seeing male homosexual preference as a problem and offering healing prayer to cure that condition); and (6) advocacy of marriage.[14]

The Million Man March, held on October 16, 1995, is the focal point of the seventh men's movement, which I call the *African American men's movement.* On that day hundreds of thousands of African American men from all over America converged on Washington, D.C. The march's beginnings were admittedly controversial because the leadership for it was provided by Louis Farrakhan, a Nation of Islam leader who has been known to make racially offensive remarks. But the march took on a power all its own. For more than seven hours the men gathered at the Lincoln Memorial for the stated purpose of pledging themselves to self-reliance and

respect for women. By their very presence they made clear
that racism and inequality cannot be ignored.
The march was also seen as a validation and vindication
of black men. Often burdened with even more stereotypes
than the rest of us males, black men had a day to show the
nation that these stereotypes were all wrong. As *Time* magazine put it, "For a day . . . all that [negative stereotyping] was
swept aside by the picture of black males urgently but peace-
fully demonstrating, in all senses of the word, their strength
and capability." It was a day when "the main point was
comradeship, pride and rededication to a few core values."[15]
Hugh Price, president of the National Urban League, suggested, "I think this may have been the largest family-values
rally in the history of America. The proof will be whether it
translates into action back home." Secretary of Housing and
Urban Development Henry Cisneros added, "Americans
know that things are profoundly wrong. The question now is
where do we go from here?"[16]

The Million Man March offered a bit of hope that through
men supporting men, a revolution toward something better
can be begun. Recent news releases give proof that this was
not just a single-day event but rather a seed for renewal.
Participants have found ways to live out the vision. In At-
lanta, a drive added 4,000 accounts to the city's four black-
owned banks. In Detroit, calls have increased dramatically
to a national clearinghouse that aids in the adoption of black
children. In Kansas City, men have volunteered to be mentors, tutors, and cafeteria monitors in the schools; have
registered voters; have organized to revamp the homes of
elderly persons; and have started a program to help city jail
inmates leave behind the lifestyles that got them behind
bars. As Nate Harris of Kansas City put it, "Once you went
on the march, you could not come back and not do anything."[17]

A Fiction Straining to Be a Fact

So far I have spoken of a number of sources of pain in men and a corresponding hunger for a movement that touches such needs. I have spoken of a range of men's movements that in various ways are ministering to men's anguish and stirring their dreams. Though these movements had different founders and purposes, they are no longer as distinct as they were in their early stages. Men may take part in several men's movements, and adherents of one often express friendly appreciation and constructive criticism of the others. Something can be learned from each of them.

I am grateful for what these men in leadership have done. After noting the creativity and energy with which women were working on their concerns, I am glad that equally gifted men are helping us sort out life for ourselves. I have read works or heard spokespersons from each of the movements I have mentioned and have been instructed by them all.

And yet none of these movements alone completely satisfies me. I hope for more freedom to experience the variety of temperaments, gifts, and skills of us men. I want our movement to make things better for all people, including our sisters, daughters, and lovers. I dream of a movement that is more multiracial and intercultural than any of the movements have yet been. I want our movement to face and take action to meet the pressing needs of our world. Although I am grateful for the impact the Christian movements have had in stirring renewed faith in men, I need a greater variety of spiritual searching and expression than I have noted in any of these thus far.

A friend who read this chapter made a similar observation. After offering several perceptive comments, he added, "I must admit that I am suspicious of all movements. Not that I object to some of the things of which they speak. I wouldn't miss a meeting of my men's group, and I want to be a good friend, husband, father. Maybe we should found a no-movement movement." Perhaps each of us will have to choose what he wants and needs from among the men's movements I have described. Yet even as I honor these

movements, I search for something more. That is their contribution to me—they stir a longing for even greater freedom
as a male to be, to become, to worship, and to contribute to a
better world.

I don't expect to start another movement with this book.
But I may offer some guidance and support for a no-movement
movement, which may become a journey of friends.

So let's explore this exciting subject together. I acknowledge
a circle of friends who have informed me and whose thoughts
I bring to this journey. These include the mentors from the
existing movements and the many men I have known as
friends, colleagues, and counselees. I also share my own
experience, including the biblical and theological resources I
have discovered thus far. Let the journey toward becoming
different kinds of men begin.

Invitations

At the end of each chapter I offer a list of possible promises,
commitments, or steps of growth you can make. I encourage
you to consider seriously which ones you want to do. Some
invitations from this chapter:

___ Learn more about one of the movements mentioned.

___ Attend a men's group or gathering.

___ Seek to know better a man whom you admire.

___ Offer friendship and support to a man who seems to be
struggling.

___ Write your own promise, commitment, or step of growth:

_____

_____

Questions for Conversation and Group Discussion

At the end of each chapter I offer questions for group discussion. Perhaps group members will read the chapter and
discuss it. Or one may read it, tell the others some of the
highlights, and invite discussion.

1. Have you been part of any of the men's movements mentioned? Which ones? What was most helpful about that experience? What was least helpful about that experience?

2. In what ways are men the most privileged people in our society? In what ways are men the least privileged people in our society? How does the church help or hinder men in their roles?

3. Where do you go to feel the support of other men? Do you find what you are looking for? In what ways? Do you feel the need for more support from other men?

4. How does your church respond to each of the movements mentioned in this chapter? How could men of your church support each other?

Resources

Balswick, Jack. *Men at the Crossroads: Beyond Traditional Roles and Modern Options.* Downers Grove, Ill.: InterVarsity Press, 1992.

Becker, Verne. "Promise Keepers: Is Their Word Really THE Word?" *Wingspan: Journal of the Male Spirit* 9, no. 2 (August–October 1995): 1, 6-7.

Bly, Robert. *Iron John: A Book about Men.* Reading, Mass.: Addison-Wesley, 1990.

Farrell, Warren. *The Myth of Male Power.* New York: Simon and Schuster, 1993.

Gilbreath, Edward. "Great Awakening: Promise Keepers' Ambitious Agenda for Transforming Christian Men." *Christianity Today* 39, no. 2 (6 February 1995): 21-28.

Goldberg, Herb. *The New Male.* New York: Signet Books, 1979.

Gurian, Michael. *The Wonder of Boys: What Parents, Mentors, and Educators Can Do to Shape Boys into Exceptional Men.* New York: Jeremy P. Tarcher/Putnam Book, 1996.

Harding, Christopher, ed. *Wingspan: Inside the Men's Movement.* New York: St. Martin's Press, 1992.

Keen, Sam. *Fire in the Belly: On Being a Man.* New York: Bantam Books, 1991.

Koepcke, Rick, and E. James Wilder. "Six Streams: Diverse Emphases within the Christian Men's Movement." *Leadership* 15, no. 3 (summer 1994): 126.

Lacayo, Richard. "We, Too, Sing America." *Time* 146, no. 44 (30 October 1995): 33-36.

Olson, Richard P. *Changing Male Roles in Today's World: A Christian Perspective for Men—and Women Who Care about Them.* Valley Forge, Pa.: Judson Press, 1982.

Pipher, Mary. *Reviving Ophelia: Saving the Selves of Adolescent Girls.* New York: Ballantine, 1994.

Sanchez, Mary. "Million Man March Was Just a Kickoff." *Kansas City Star,* Metro section (26 January 1996): 1C, 8C.

Notes

1. Mary Pipher, *Reviving Ophelia* (New York: Ballantine, 1994).
2. Michael Gurian, *The Wonder of Boys* (New York: Jeremy P. Tarcher/Putnam Book, 1996).
3. Warren Farrell, *The Myth of Male Power* (New York: Simon and Schuster, 1993).
4. Jack Balswick, *Men at the Crossroads* (Downers Grove, Ill.: InterVarsity Press, 1992), 36.
5. Herb Goldberg, *The New Male* (New York: Signet Books, 1979).
6. Richard P. Olson, *Changing Male Roles in Today's World* (Valley Forge, Pa.: Judson Press, 1982).
7. Robert Bly, *Iron John: A Book about Men* (Reading, Mass.: Addison-Wesley, 1990).
8. Sam Keen, *Fire in the Belly* (New York: Bantam Books, 1991).
9. Balswick, *Men at the Crossroads*, 38.
10. Christopher Harding, ed., *Wingspan* (New York: St. Martin's Press, 1992), xiii-xv.
11. Verne Becker, "Promise Keepers: Is Their Word Really THE Word?" *Wingspan* 9, no. 2 (August-October 1995): 1, 6.
12. Ibid., 6.
13. Edward Gilbreath, "Great Awakening: Promise Keepers' Ambitious Agenda for Transforming Christian Men," *Christianity Today* 39, no. 2 (6 February 1995): 23.
14. Rick Koepcke and E. James Wilder, "Six Streams: Diverse Emphases within the Christian Men's Movement," *Leadership* 15, no. 3 (summer 1994): 126.
15. Richard Lacayo, "We, Too, Sing America," *Time* 146, no. 44 (30 October 1995): 34, 35.
16. Ibid., 34.
17. Mary Sanchez, "Million Man March Was Just a Kickoff," *Kansas City Star,* Metro section (26 January 1996): 1C, 8C.

2

Our Search for Role and Soul

We men are often more interested in doing the task at hand than in reflecting on who we are. We don't often spend much time critiquing the culture of which we are a part. Much less do we talk about what male roles are and why they are what they are.

It has been said that the last thing a fish would study is water! We are rather like those fish, simply living in the water. Once in a while, however, we should test the water. Is it healthy, wholesome, life-supporting? Or has it become polluted and poisoned?

Some of our gifted brothers and sisters are asking those questions about culture and its impact on male roles. Indeed, a huge amount of information and opinion exists on this subject. I try in this chapter to sort out and summarize what seems most important. In this summary, I hope neither to oversimplify nor to drive you away with too much detail. The issue of cultural roles is but one of the doors into greater male self-awareness and health, so consider it in as much depth and detail as fits your need.

A fascinating Bible story from David's early life gives us a handle for considering this issue. The youthful David has been sent by his father, Jesse, to take food supplies to his three older brothers who are serving in King Saul's army and to King Saul himself. While visiting the camp, David hears the taunts of the Philistine giant, Goliath. This giant's "height was six cubits and a span. He had a helmet of bronze on his head, and he was armed with a coat of mail; the weight of the coat was five thousand shekels of bronze [125 pounds]. He had greaves [coverings] of bronze on his legs and a javelin of bronze slung between his shoulders. The shaft of his spear was like a weaver's beam, and his spear's head weighed six hundred shekels of iron [fifteen pounds]. . ." (1 Samuel 17:5-7).

Repeatedly, Goliath would come within clear sight and sound of the Israelites' camp and shout a challenge: "Today I defy the ranks of Israel! Give me a man, that we may fight together. . . . Choose a man for yourselves, and let him come down to me. If he is able to fight with me and kill me, then we will be your servants; but if I prevail against him and kill him, then you shall be our servants and serve us" (vv. 10, 8-9). This bold challenge intimidated Saul and his troops, who were "dismayed and greatly afraid" (v. 11).

To everyone's surprise, David, the youthful shepherd, volunteers to fight Goliath. King Saul resists, telling him, "you are just a boy, and he has been a warrior from his youth" (v. 33). David assures him that he has faced bears and lions as a shepherd and that the God who delivered him before will deliver him in this crisis. In desperation Saul accepts David's brave offer. And then he equips the young shepherd: "he put a bronze helmet on his head and clothed him with a coat of mail. David strapped Saul's sword over the armor, and he tried in vain to walk, for he was not used to them" (vv. 38-39).

So David takes off the other man's armor. It does not fit him, nor does it fit his way of doing battle. Rather he faces the enemy his way, carrying his staff, five smooth stones in his pouch, his sling in his hand. And he prevails! With his sling, he hurls a well-aimed stone that strikes the giant in the forehead. Goliath falls and is defeated (vv. 41-51).

For now, let's take just one discovery from this story. For David to succeed in the frightening and daunting task before him, he could not wear the armor of someone else. He could not fit the style, the expectations, the role that others laid on him. He had to look within—to himself and to his God—for his true way. Only then could he triumph in a perilous time. That story rose in my memory as I pondered the issues we are concerned with here. Like David, each of us has some scary tasks to accomplish. We too are offered the armor, the structures, the ways of doing things that others have used. These ways are customary and have guided men in the past. As David sorted, decided, rejected, and chose what fit him, so must we choose or else we lose our soul. And as David succeeded in what he was called to do, so may we.

David's dilemma was different from ours, however. The armor offered him was visible; the armor offered us is invisible. Saul's helmet and coat of mail came to David from the outside, and they were not his size. They did not fit. They were strange and foreign to him. The "armor" offered us is so much a part of our ways of doing things that we don't even recognize it. Much of it is so widely accepted that we don't know it's there. If we feel discomfort, we are apt to think that something is wrong with us rather than with the armor, the roles and expectations we are expected to fulfill.

The armor of the male role to which we are expected to conform shows up in statements and questions that may make us uncomfortable. For example, "Are you a man?"— the question Lady MacBeth asked her husband. Or, "Are you man enough?"—to fight or play football or seduce a woman and so on. Or, "Come on, little boy, be a man!" or an army recruiting slogan, "A man's got to do what a man's got to do."

If we are to choose freely what is fitting for what we are called to do and be, we need to recognize what is laid on us from the outside. And we need to balance those expectations with what comes from inside—what are our "givens"—anatomy, genetics, gifts, disposition, and more. In short, we need to search for our role and our soul. We need to sort out and then accept or reject others' expectations. And we need to look for the core of our spiritual and moral self, our soul.

This is difficult work! To help you discover who you truly are so that, to use another army recruiting phrase, you can "be all that you can be," I explore a series of questions.

What Are Traditional American Role Expectations for Men, and Do They Still Fit?

In *The Forty-Nine Percent Majority,* Deborah S. David and Robert Brannon explore the traditional role expectations for American males. Although no single model of what it means to be a male in our society exists, they note four general themes.

The first theme is "No Sissy Stuff." A stigma is attached to anything that seems even remotely feminine, and this stigma surfaces in every aspect of a man's life. Men are told, Don't smell like a woman; buy a deodorant or cologne only if it has a vigorous, macho name. Don't choose typical women's vocabulary, foods, or occupations. Don't engage in "women's hobbies" such as knitting, flower arranging, or doing needlepoint. Further, don't admit to loving art, poetry, music, fine arts, dance. Don't be open or vulnerable, and above all, don't cry. Don't reveal your intimate thoughts, searchings, uncertainties. Don't express affection to other males, and certainly not with hugs or kisses.

The second theme they note is "The Big Wheel." Men need success and status; they need to be looked up to or admired, to feel like a success. Usually this success is defined in terms of money, power, and prestige, and it's nice if they fit together somehow. Because few men will experience success by these standards, we look for alternate routes. We may want to display symbols of success in the things we buy (a car or a stereo, for example). Or we may enjoy being the best at something, anything. For example, one may tremendously enjoy being the champion dart thrower, the best ballplayer, the fastest mail sorter.

Another aspect of the need to be successful is the need to be competent, to project the impression that "I don't need any help." So often, we men have a hard time admitting that we don't know something or that we need help. We will walk around grocery stores rather than ask a clerk for the location of an item. We may be hopelessly lost on the road, but we keep on driving, hoping to find a way to solve our lostness ourselves. (A joke puts it this way: "Why does it take a half million sperm to get one ovum fertilized? The sperm won't ask for directions!") We risk our backs carrying heavy burdens that could be balanced much more easily between two people. And far too often, we struggle alone with personal problems and anxiety that could be much more easily borne if shared with a friend or counselor.

Another important way to feel like a success is to be the "breadwinner" for one's family. And yet in a time when it is necessary for both partners in many marriages to earn paychecks, this avenue to being a success, a "big wheel" if you will, is cut off as well.

The third theme, closely related to the second, is "The Sturdy Oak." Men are to develop a "manly air of toughness, confidence, and self-reliance," a style of thinking for oneself, of being serious and unconquerable. Strength, independence, calmness, indeed fearlessness, even in the face of pain, danger, death—these are the marks of the man who is a "Sturdy Oak."

We may attempt to express this aspect through physical strength or athletic prowess. Or we may attempt to show it through toughness on the job. But in truth, the feelings of most of us flesh-and-blood males do not conform to this "Sturdy Oak" image. If we attempt to conform to it, we may well act in ways that don't fit who we really are. If we allow this expectation to dominate us, we may experience much inner strain.

The fourth theme is "Give 'em Hell!"—an "aura of aggression, violence, and daring." David and Brannon point out there is nothing inherently wrong with embodying the first three themes. Being a success or having confidence and determination or earning respect can be very good. It may be oppressive to *have* to do these things all the time, but for the most part these goals are wholesome.

This fourth theme, however, is neither wholesome nor constructive. It involves the need to hurt, to embarrass, to punish, to defeat, to humble, to outwit others. For us males, the term *aggressive* is generally taken to be a compliment. Surprisingly, it is seldom questioned. We males know better and feel differently about those we love. And yet, set up a competition with another male, and we immediately try to "give' em hell!"

This theme can show up in the desire for reckless adventure and daring—perhaps driving high-powered cars at high speeds, perhaps taking chances with alcohol or other drugs. Sexual aggressiveness is also a part of this theme. Men may see in themselves a dangerous tendency to want to overpower a desirable woman rather than enter into an equal, mutually consenting relationship. Aggressiveness and violence seem to be part of the male role.

David and Brannon note how these four themes fit together:

> All together and in its purest form, the male sex role depicts a rather remarkable creature. This hypothetical man never feels anxious, depressed, or vulnerable, has never known the taste of tears, is devoid of any trace or hint of femininity. He is looked up to by all who know him, is a tower of strength both physically and emotionally, and exudes an unshakable confidence and determination that sets him apart from lesser beings. He's also aggressive, forceful, and daring, a barely controlled volcano of primal force.[1]

They wrote this powerful analysis twenty years ago. I'd like to think that both society and each of us have changed a great deal since then. However, these expectations continue to exert a very strong influence. Of course, all of us can locate places where these descriptions do not fit us. It may be more helpful, however, to ask another question. That is, where do they accurately describe what is expected and how we act?

As I became aware of these role expectations for us men, I noted at least five things that are very difficult for us men to say:

1. I don't know.
2. I made a mistake; I was wrong.
3. I need help.
4. I am afraid. (It is difficult to say I *feel* anything, but to recognize and admit fear is probably the most difficult of all.)
5. I am sorry.[2]

And there may be a sixth: Help me understand.

If I find it difficult or impossible to say these things, I am cut off from the possibilities for much growth and learning, from important parts of myself, and from people. My greatest hope in my life for closeness with those I love most is hampered by these difficulties. There is much about traditional American male role expectations it will be good to shed, if only we can!

Are Biology and Anatomy Our Determinants?

Some believe that the behaviors of males I have just described are natural and inevitable because of differences between men's and women's bodies and body chemistry. Men's bodies, on the average, are larger than women's. Men's bodies provide sperm so that women's bodies may conceive. Men's bodies cannot conceive, give birth, or nurse the newborn. These facts will influence what is asked of men and of women at given points in their lives.

Beyond these, do other biological factors influence or determine male roles? Melvin Konner, a biological anthropologist, has investigated this in his book *The Tangled Wing*. After exploring the latest scientific and clinical evidence, Konner concludes that testosterone, the main male sex hormone, predisposes men to a slightly higher level of aggressiveness than females. But, he adds, biology does not determine all of our behavior, or even much of it.[3] Other explanations for the distinct gender role expectations can be given.

Is There a Universal Cultural Expectation for Males?

If we could look at all the cultures of the world, would we find unanimous agreement about what role men are expected to play in their various cultures? Anthropologist David D. Gilmore explored that question and reported his findings in *Manhood in the Making,* subtitled *Cultural Concepts of Masculinity.* Gilmore set out to examine these issues: "Is there a deep structure of manhood? Is there a global archetype of manliness?"[4] Among most of the cultures he studied, he found that "true manhood is a precious and elusive status beyond mere maleness. There is a male image that men and boys aspire to, one that their culture demands of them as a measure of belonging."[5]

Further, in each of these cultures, some men fail the culture's test for manhood. These become negative examples, the men-who-are-not-men. Such examples are held up to inspire conformity to that culture's ideal of manhood. For example, in Chinese culture a male suffering from the condition called *koro* may display a number of symptoms including acute anxiety, palpitations, trembling, and the experience of intimations of impending death. These men suffer an "overriding fear that manhood is taking flight."[6] The usual victim of this condition is a young or adolescent man with a weak or dependent personality, perhaps with poor education, perhaps painfully shy, who feels he cannot live up to the standards of performance his culture sets up for him. Thus *koro* may be seen as a male hysteria, a reaction to the pressures a young male may feel for achieving masculinity.

Becoming a man, therefore, is by no means automatic. Gilmore discovered in the cultures he studied a "constant recurring notion that real manhood is different from simple anatomical maleness."[7] It is a desired state that boys must attain against powerful odds. In practically all of the societies studied, "Manhood ideologies force men to shape up on penalty of being robbed of their identity, a threat apparently worse than death."[8]

Things work differently for females, Gilmore notes. The adult female status is more often *ascribed,* but the adult male status is more often *achieved.* As anthropologist Gilbert Herdt has written, "Femininity unfolds naturally, whereas masculinity must be achieved; and here is where the male ritual cult steps in."[9] The young male must overcome obstacles in order to become a man, and must perform certain duties to become a worthy man. Norman Mailer spoke for many cultures when he wrote, "Nobody was born a man; you attained manhood provided you were good enough, bold enough."[10]

What was expected of a man in all these societies? There were three imperatives: He was to be impregnator, protector, and provider. Most societies were dangerous or highly competitive, and so to fulfill these roles involved much risk and demanded courage. Men are asked to make a moral commitment to defend the society and its core values against all odds. As contrasted to a child, a man is expected to produce more than he consumes and to give more than he takes.

Indeed, this is one of the surprises of Gilmore's study. When he began his investigation, he was prepared to confirm that conventional femininity is nurturing and that masculinity is self-serving, egotistical, and uncaring. But he did not find that at all. Rather, he found that the notion of manhood in virtually all cultures includes a criterion of "selfless generosity even to the point of sacrifice. Real men are generous, even to a fault. . . ."[11] It is the nonmen who are stigmatized as lazy, stingy, unproductive. Male nurturing may be different from female nurturing, but nurturing is indeed a criterion for manhood.

Although these three responsibilities (begetting children, protecting, and providing) are constant, they may be achieved in various ways. In Japan, for example, there is a "hard" way to be a man and a "soft" way. The hard way is the way of the warrior: the martial arts expert, the samurai warrior, the sumo wrestler, the kamikaze pilot. The soft way is epitomized by the famous Japanese film hero Tora-San. Tora-San, probably the most beloved character in the history of Japanese film, is a wandering do-gooder with a pacifist bent. This noble, gentle adventurer helps the weak, solves problems, and upholds the family virtues of his society. The soft way is a way of duty, caring, and social responsibility.

Quite similar expectations define and guide those who want to be men in the vast majority of cultures—but not quite all. Gilmore located at least two cultures with quite different expectations. One was found on the island of Tahiti. There, sex differences are not strongly marked; men and woman are seen as having similar personalities. Further, the roles and tasks of men and women are almost indistinguishable. Both do most of the tasks, and all jobs and skills are open to persons of either gender. Quite frequently men do the cooking, and women do almost everything that men do outside the house. In this culture, the need to prove manhood or the pressure for men to establish themselves as significantly different from women or children is absent.

In Tahiti there is no warfare or feuding with other tribes, and fish and farmable lands are plentiful. The economy does not promote competitiveness among men but fosters cooperation. Families assist each other in food gathering. The culture does not promote achieving or striving or gaining more material goods than one's family needs.[12]

The other culture that displayed different cultural expectations was that of the Semai, one of the aboriginal peoples of Southeast Asia. The Semai, who currently live in the mountains of the Malay peninsula, are a people nonaggressive to the core.

> The Semai believe that to resist advances from another person, sexual or otherwise, is equivalent to aggression against that person. They call such aggressiveness *puna*—a very important concept in their culture, meaning roughly "taboo." Puna is a Semai word for any act, no matter how mild, that denies or frustrates another person. The Semai believe that if you puna someone,

his/her "heart becomes heavy" and the affected person may therefore hurt himself or become disoriented and do something inappropriate or even violent.[13]

This strong prohibition against aggressiveness applies equally to men, women, and children. The Semai personality has a pervasive nonviolent self-image. Like the Tahitians, the Semai share practically all work, with little sex differentiation. The men do like to hunt, using blow guns, and delight in these weapons, but the hunting is not essential to maintaining their diet. Cooperation, nonviolence, avoiding or running away from harsh conflict are all norms in this society.[14]

Why are there such different expectations of males in these two cultures as contrasted to most of the rest of the world? Gilmore suggests two possible and interrelated explanations. Humans have two possible responses to danger: flight or fight. The Tahitians and the Semai have developed a "flight" response; all the others resort to a "fight" response. Further, expectations of males may be connected to the harshness of the surroundings. If there is a struggle to provide, and if there is threat and danger from outside, the male must perhaps be more harshly socialized to call forth the qualities needed. In a benign atmosphere with little threat from without and abundance within this harsh socialization is not necessary. Gilmore reflects on his findings:

What do the exceptional cases, the gentle Tahitians and the timid Semai, show about masculinity? Most importantly they suggest that . . . manliness is a symbolic script, a cultural construct, endlessly variable and not always necessary.[15]

Does this statement imply that our Western masculinity is a fraud, unnecessary and dispensable? Could it be thrown away? Could men instead be playful Peter Pans, devoted to self-fulfillment and sensitivity? Or is there something about our complex and competitive world that demands the tough disciplines usually found in a manhood-of-achievement ethic?

And Gilmore raises an even more significant question: Why do we have to be competitive or disciplined at all? Could a modern industrial society exist without an aggressive masculine gender role?

As interesting as these questions are, Gilmore reminds us, "We do not make up our roles from scratch. The possibilities are not limitless. So long as there are battles to be fought, wars to be won, heights to be scaled, hard work to be done, some of us will have to 'act like men.'"[16] And then he asks, why should women be excluded from these challenges with their corresponding satisfactions?

Gilmore's thorough study answers some questions but raises even more provocative ones.

Is There Something Universal about Maleness Itself?

A number of people in the new men's movement urge us to look not at culture but at the male personality itself to discover what it means to be men. For example, Robert Moore and Douglas Gillette suggest, "It is our experience that deep within every man are blueprints, what we can also call 'hard wiring' for the calm and positive mature masculine."[17] These blueprints are what psychologist Carl Jung called archetypes. He believed that these archetypes provide the very foundations of our behaviors, our thinking, our feeling, our characteristic human reactions. Some believe it quite possible that we inherit these archetypes genetically. The existence of these blueprints or archetypes is seen both in the analysis of night dreams and daydreams and in-depth studies of literature, legends, and mythology the world over.

Moore and Gillette point to four archetypes of mature masculine energies: king, warrior, magician, and lover. These all overlap and enrich one another. I would note, though, that males and females have both their own and the other sex's archetypes. In the following, we describe nothing that is unavailable to females. We simply describe some inherent claims on us as males. Also, each archetype has boyish or immature versions, as well as manly or mature versions. Further, each archetype may be expressed either in its rich fullness or in a dysfunctional way. And so in each, we see something that inspires and guides and something that warns, something to avoid. Let's take a look at each in this light.

The *king* energy reflects the image of God—good judgment, wisdom, selflessness. The mature king is regenerative as he performs two functions. One is to *order reality*. The king orders reality within himself by maintaining the balance between the warrior, the magician, and the lover. In other words, the king first models order in his own life and then provides it to other areas within his responsibility. This activity suggests the qualities of rational and reasonable patterning, of integrity and integration, of stability and centeredness, of maintaining balance. Second, the king provides *fertility* and *blessing*. Children are born, and those whose life the king touches are encouraged and affirmed.

If the king in the male psyche is not mature, the king may fall into being an aggressive tyrant on the one hand or a dependent weakling on the other. The good king avoids those perils and seeks a healthy balance.

Then there is the *warrior*. Though this image makes many of us uncomfortable, it needs to be considered. As Jack Balswick notes, "Attempting to deny or repress the warrior archetype within men is merely to invite it to resurface in another form—as emotional and physical violence. Rightly understood, the good warrior is a necessary part of every healthy male psyche."[18]

The healthy mature warrior will attempt to do something about life's tasks and problems. He will have good reason and sound strategy. He endures training to be well prepared, accepts self-discipline, and is in control of his body and mind. Further, the warrior commits to something beyond himself, to a higher cause. A warrior knows that this commitment may cost him everything, including his life; he knows how few his days are. Rather than depressing him, this awareness leads him to pour out his lifeforce and to experience life fiercely in a way unknown to others.[19] Courage, skill, self-discipline, awareness of the frailty of life—these are the qualities of the mature warrior.

Some point out that this image, though rooted in war, can be applied to a variety of causes and needs. These same qualities can help one provide for a family or complete a course of study or serve valiantly in a humanitarian effort or on a mission field. Book titles such as *The Tender Warrior* and *Knights without Armor* suggest that this image is better reapplied to new causes than totally abandoned.[20]

Of course, there is also great danger in the immature warrior. On the one extreme there is the masochist, who enjoys suffering; on the other there is the sadist, who enjoys inflicting suffering. The warrior instinct must be controlled and held in close contact with the other archetypes.

The third archetype is the *magician.* In the magician's energy is awareness and insight, the knowing and mastering of technology. This type is coming into its own these days with the rise of computer technology. Technology wizards like Bill Gates amass great wealth and have tremendous power to influence and change their world.

The magician possesses the power of observation and the ability to make adjustments. He sees into the depths both of nature and of human beings and thus has the power to deflate arrogance. Thoughtfulness, discernment, and reflection are the magician's gifts. Further, the magician is an initiator who offers the rituals that bring young men into the secrets of maturity. The magician is guru, mentor, teacher.

In immaturity, a magician may be the detached operator, one who employs his secret information to manipulate others rather than help them. Many a movie theme these days draws on a fear of the evil computer manipulator.

The fourth archetype is the *lover,* the one who is the master of play, the exemplar of healthy embodiment, of being in the world, of sensuousness without shame. The lover wants to touch and be touched, both physically and emotionally. The lover affirms his sex, sexuality, and sexual passions. (Too often, this aspect of the lover has been misdirected, both by the church and by the culture. So we will return to the calling of sexuality and sensuousness in the closing chapter.)

The lover's energy is also the source of spirituality. The lover feels a longing for the divine, a mystical bent; he is eager for oneness with God and with all things. The lover feels the pain and poignancy of the world but experiences its great joy as well. The mature lover is earthy and spiritual, feeling great sorrow and great happiness.

Of course, immature lovers are in ample supply. On the one hand, the addicted lover wants the pleasure of love without its commitment and cost. On the other hand, the impotent lover experiences life unfeelingly, lacking its aliveness.

Besides these four basic and most frequently mentioned archetypes, there are others, of which I will briefly mention just three.

Aaron Kipnis reminds us of the *trickster* archetype,

> a mythological figure present in almost every culture, present and past. Almost always male, he represents a complex aspect of the psyche. He is paradoxical, uncontrollable, iconoclastic, and in many ways difficult to fathom. He is playful and spontaneous. As a breaker of boundaries he tends to deflate those who are pompous, egoistic, controlling, dominating, and inflated.[21]

Kipnis saw this archetype at play in a group of which he was a part. He saw it particularly in their humor, when they would "goad, tease, and jive one another with parody, satire, and black humor."[22] He notes that men often use laughter to heal the shame of their worst failures. Tricksters, he observes, defeat the ego in the service of the self. They shock people out of self-satisfaction, dull routine, unexamined habits. Thus the trickster is the stimulus both to creativity and to peacemaking.

Yet another archetype is the *wild man,* a person alone, close to nature. "He is a deep soulful being, close to animals and forest life," a type that we ignored as we moved toward urban living.[23] This lonely, untamed person, living from the provisions of nature and more in tune with it than with other humans, is a frequent figure in American folklore. And yet it is one we have repressed and ignored, to our great loss. Henry David Thoreau was perhaps one of our last "wild men." Somehow we need to call forth intellectual wild men, urban wild men, churchgoing wild men.

One other archetype is the *green man*. This is the masculine personification of nature, the male counterpart to "mother earth." Like the wild man, the green man is aware of the beauty and power of nature and has an earthy, passionate commitment to creation. He urges us to live in ways that bring health to our lives, families, communities, and environment.[24]

These archetypes form a whole. Each of the archetypes checks and balances the others. If I am controlled by one of these to the exclusion of the others, I will be unbalanced and will lack wholeness and centeredness.

The existence of these archetypes does not mean that we will end as clones of each other. We will vary in how we live out the various aspects and which are most prominent in our lives. All of us will be stronger in one or two than we are in the others. Nonetheless, we are well reminded to attend to all of them, to cultivate and call forth those that are weakest in our lives.

Jack Balswick believes that the major imbalance among men today is in the lover archetype. The king, warrior, and magician harmonize with each other and fit together quite easily. And yet, unless the lover is added, a man leads an existence that is detached from others and from life. "Men today are specialists in detachment," Balswick observes; "we need to know how to overcome this detachment and become more connected to other people."[25] Giving attention to the lover archetype energizes the other aspects of our being and also humanizes them.

This, then, is the answer from the mythopoetic men's movement to our quest: if we want to know what is truly male, we should look for the blueprint inside, to be discovered in dreams and in ancient literature, and live it out maturely in a manner that fits us.

How Does a Boy Become a Man?
Is Initiation Necessary?

In the movie *The Emerald Forest,* a white boy, Tommy, has been captured and raised by a Brazilian tribe. One day as he is playing in the river with a beautiful girl—with growing sexual interest — the chief, some tribal elders, and the chief's wife come upon Tommy, surprising him. The chief booms out, "Tommy, your time has come to die!" Everyone appears profoundly shaken. The chief's wife plays the part of all women and mothers and asks, "Must he die?" The chief answers with a threatening "yes." Then is portrayed a night ritual in which Tommy is apparently tortured by the older men in the tribe. He is forced into forest vines, where his flesh is attacked by jungle ants. He struggles in agony, his body mutilated by the ants.

When the sun finally rises, Tommy is taken down to the river by the men and bathed; the clinging ants are washed from his body. Then the chief calls out, "The boy is dead, and the man is born!" The initiation is not over, for Tommy is guided into a spiritual experience, induced by a drug blown through a long pipe into his nose. As he hallucinates, he discovers his animal soul (an eagle) and soars above the world. Then he is a man. He is permitted to marry, to take on man's responsibilities as a brave in the tribe, and eventually to become chief.[26]

This movie portrays a male ritual of initiation into manhood. Arnold van Gennep wrote of his in his classic work, first published in 1908. According to van Gennep, the underlying theme of such rites is the male's change in status and identity. As in the movie, the boy "dies" and is "reborn" a man. There are three stages: (1) *separation,* in which the boy severs relations with childhood, perhaps by renouncing his mother or by being forcibly taken away from her; (2) *transition,* when he is sent away to a new place or is isolated and remains in limbo, neither boy nor man but something in between; and (3) *incorporation,* where he finally emerges and is considered a man.[27] In this initiation, often the boy must achieve some task to show that he can make a contribution to his society. For example, in some of the groups Gilmore studied, a boy was not considered a man until he made his first hunting kill or proved his ability as a herdsman.

Many in the new men's movement find something vital and important in this concept of initiation. Robert Bly has described the earning of manhood as a four-stage initiation process that boys go through again and again: (1) The boy must feel his mother's love and blessing, and then he must leave her. (2) He must also feel his father's love and blessing, and then he must leave him. He will go alone into the forest or the unconscious or the unmapped world to pursue his manhood. (3) He will find spiritual elders, or mentors, or "male mothers," who will guide and initiate him. And finally, (4) he will pass "beyond the realm of the personal mother and father" to achieve "spiritual mating with the universe."[28]

Moore and Gillette point out that two things are needed for these rituals to ring true: first, a sacred space is necessary, a place ritually hallowed and set aside for this purpose. Second, the ritual requires an elder, a wise old man or wise old woman "who is completely trustworthy and can lead the initiate through the process and deliver him (or her) intact and enhanced on the other side."[29]

But our society doesn't have these things now and perhaps never did; and thoughtful men like Moore and Gillette point out that we need to take very seriously the disappearance of such ritual processes, such initiations. Why is this vital process so scarce? Perhaps the Protestant Reformation and the Enlightenment discouraged and discredited the process. Perhaps becoming an adult male in contemporary society is such a complex and gradual process that the notion of a distinct event to mark it fell out of favor. Gilmore quotes Thomas De Quincey: "But when, by what test, by what indication does manhood commence? Physically by one criterion, legally by another. Morally by a third, intellectually by a fourth—and all indefinite."[30] I would add, occupationally by a fifth criterion, and spiritually by a sixth, and, indeed, all these are indefinite and incomplete.

Ask a group of men, "When did you feel you had become a man?" and you will hear a variety of answers: When I joined the army, when I went away to college, when I graduated from college, when I got my first job, when I first made love, when I married, when my first child was born. Some might give an answer from their religious experience. One Jewish man recalled, "On my Bar Mitzvah day, I heard the words, 'Today you are a man!' The next day, however, I was still my parents' little boy." Christians may recall the day of their confirmation or believer's baptism and realize that, however profound a religious experience it was, it was a very incomplete initiation into manhood.

Moore and Gillette observe that we are currently stuck with what they call pseudo-initiations. Examples might be initiation into a gang, a fraternity, military service. Or perhaps we experience no initiation at all. The consequence is dire: a predominance of what they call "boy psychology," dangerous immaturity rather than the mature manhood our culture so desperately needs.

We are left with a troubling question: how do we help boys develop into mature, great-hearted men? Where is our presence and help needed?

What Perspectives Does the Christian Faith Offer?

As persons of faith, how are we to see this issue? Let's begin by looking at the male archetypes. One probably would not arrive at this understanding of maleness reading the Scriptures. However, it is interesting to look at men in Scriptures after hearing about the archetypes. We can find examples of each in the Bible.

Concerning the king archetype, we are told of David, who accepted and fulfilled the role, of Saul and Solomon, who each in some way fell short of it. After the kingdom divided, the Bible lists large numbers of kings; a few were faithful, but many were not. We are also given examples of persons who rose above dire circumstances to give kingly guidance, leadership, and power, such as Nehemiah.

The warrior archetype is also present. We recall the opening story of this chapter, that of the brave young David facing the fierce Goliath. The stories of Samson, Abner, and Joab remind us of the violent excesses that tempt warriors when this is the main or sole archetype by which they live. In the New Testament, the warrior and armor images are applied to the Christian's battle against evil and temptation in the struggle to be God's person (Ephesians 6:13).

The magician archetype is a little more difficult to locate. Within the Bible, the term *magician* describes persons who draw upon spiritual powers that are opposed to God.[31] In the broader sense, however, the figure of the magician as one who gains knowledge and wisdom and uses reflective thought is found in the Bible. Stu Weber, author of *Tender Warrior,* uses the term *mentor* for this archetype. The "Wisdom literature" contains all the practical wisdom of the book of Proverbs and sober reflection on life found in Ecclesiastes.

The lover archetype is also present. Stu Weber uses the term *friend,* interpreting the term *lover* in its most complete sense. The deep love and friendship of Jonathan and David, the tender bond between Paul and Timothy, the guidance to love God, neighbor, spouse, and children—this is a prominent and foundational archetype in Scripture.

The less prominent archetypes may be found in Scripture as well. Consider the trickster. When the prophet Nathan told King David a story that convicted him of his sin of taking another's wife, or when Elijah confronted King Ahab in a vineyard for which he had murdered, each performed the role of trickster. They broke boundaries, they confronted, they pricked pretensions. The Bible speaks of God laughing in the heavens at the pretensions of humankind—a suggestion that God is the ultimate trickster!

Or think about the wild man. The Bible has many—Ishmael, Esau, Samson, Amos, Elijah, John the Baptist. All of these have the characteristics of wild men, "unowned, unmanipulated, unbowed, unbeholden, undomesticated, unapologetic, and unashamed."[32] Each of these wild men served God in his own way.

The green man is not as easily identified (Adam may be one), and yet much Scripture speaks of creation with great love; it is seen as a trust from God and evidence of the majesty of God, for example, Psalm 8, 19, and 24.

Jesus, the founder of our faith, powerfully embodied these archetypes. He was King, Messiah, the Anointed One. He was the secure and serene king, in contrast to the fearful and hate-driven King Herod who tried to kill him. The kingly powers of generativity and generosity resided in him. He redefined kingship and came as a servant king.

Jesus was a mature warrior. He took a stand, faced his foes, drove unjust people out of the temple. He lived under discipline and was obedient to God's will, even when, as in Gethsemane, he would have preferred something other for himself. He knew the shortness of his days and tried to prepare his disciples for this fact. He was obedient, even unto death.

Jesus was a magician mentor. He called disciples, trained them for action, sent them out to practice what he taught, and led them into further reflection and discovery. He was a careful observer of the birds of the air and lilies of the field, of planting and harvesting, and he used these everyday realities to teach about God's provision and care.

Jesus was a lover. He wept over Jerusalem and at the grave of Lazarus. He responded joyously to children. He loved deeply and inspired deep loyalty among those close to him. He reminded followers of his deep love, calling them friends, and gave a new commandment that we love one another.

We can also see Jesus as trickster. Certainly he challenged the pretensions of those around him, particularly the Pharisees, and some of his hyperboles ripple with humor (for instance, that of a camel going through the eye of a needle). He was wild man and green man, fasting in the wilderness and often withdrawing to isolated spots in nature to pray and be renewed.

These discoveries out of the Scriptures remind us men that we may have great freedom in arriving at a fitting, soulful male role for each of us. We may choose our main emphasis from among many aspects of maleness. Each aspect is to be tempered and balanced by the others.

To be faithful, the Christian man will seek above all to be lover. God's love in sending Christ, Christ's love and sacrificial death for us all, the call to love as we have been loved— these are predominant motifs for all Christians, including us males. We may need to devote particular energy to cultivating it, given that the warrior archetype also beckons.

Do We Need a New Pattern for Men?

Up to this point, everything in this chapter has described our heritage and history. However, we stand on the brink of a new millennium. We live in a technological culture, an urban culture, and a crowded world. We face the problems of pollution and poverty and fatherless children. This world is so different from that world of hunters and farmers in which these archetypes arose and male role expectations were worked out. Do we need a new understanding of the kind of man that is needed for such an age?

Our Christian faith teaches at least two truths in the face of such a question. On the one hand, God often calls people to listen to the needs and the cries of people in their own culture. Then we are to ask, what kind of men are needed in this new age? And what is my personal call in the midst of all this? As James Russell Lowell put it in the hymn "Once to Every Man and Nation," "New occasions teach new duties. Time makes ancient truth uncouth."

On the other hand, Christians are called not only to respond to the needs of their culture but to change the culture as well! In Romans 12:2, we are told, "Do not be conformed to this world [or age], but be transformed by the renewing of your minds, so that you may discern what is the will of God—what is good and acceptable and perfect." Therefore, we are called to do our part to respond to culture's needs but also to question and participate in the transforming of culture itself.

We may very well discover that we need a different kind of man for this task. In the next four chapters we will be considering various aspects of men's issues. And then in the closing two chapters, we will consider in more detail what this new man might be.

Invitations

From the above discussion, you may be identifying some areas of discovery or growth or some promises you want to make. Here are some possible invitations from this chapter:

__ Discover some male role expectations that do not fit you and to which you do not wish to conform any longer.

__ Try doing some of the things that have been traditional male "no-no's" (see the discussion of "No Sissy Stuff," p. 20).

__ Search for the king, the warrior, the magician-mentor, the lover-friend—and the trickster, wild man, and green man within yourself.

__ Pick two new ways to express the lover-friend in yourself and try them out.

__ Discover ways to welcome or initiate boys, adolescents, and young adults into mature and comfortable manhood.

__ Write your own:

_____

_____

Questions for Conversation and Group Discussion

1. When did you first feel you were a man? Did a particular occasion or accomplishment prompt this feeling? If so, what was it?

2. What ideas about male roles in this chapter felt comfortable or familiar? Do you want to question any of the ideas expressed ?

3. What ideas about male roles in this chapter felt uncomfortable or unfamiliar? Do you want to give more thought and attention to any of these?

4. Should a Christian man be different from other men? If so, in what ways?

5. Can Christian men help initiate boys into mature Christian manhood? If so, in what ways?

Resources

Balswick, Jack. *Men at the Crossroads: Beyond Traditional Roles and Modern Options.* Downers Grove, Ill.: InterVarsity Press, 1992.

Bly, Robert. *Iron John: A Book about Men.* Reading, Mass.: Addison-Wesley, 1990.

David, Deborah S., and Robert Brannon, eds. *The Forty-Nine Percent Majority.* Reading, Mass.: Addison-Wesley, 1976.

Gilmore, David D. *Manhood in the Making: Cultural Concepts of Masculinity.* New Haven: Yale University Press, 1990.

Harding, Christopher, ed. *Wingspan: Inside the Men's Movement.* New York: St. Martin's Press, 1992.

Keen, Sam. *Fire in the Belly: On Being a Man.* New York: Bantam Books, 1991.

Kipnis, Aaron R. *Knights without Armor: A Practical Guide for Men in Quest of Masculine Soul.* New York: Jeremy P. Tarcher/Putnam Book, G. P. Putnam's Sons, 1991.

Moore, Robert, and Douglas Gillette. *King, Warrior, Magician, Lover.* San Francisco: Harper, 1990.

Olson, Richard P. *Changing Male Roles in Today's World: A Christian Perspective for Men—and Women Who Care about Them.* Valley Forge, Pa.: Judson Press, 1982.

Pittman, Frank, III. *Man Enough.* New York: G. P. Putnam's Sons, 1993.

Weber, Stu. *Tender Warrior: God's Intention for a Man.* Sisters, Oreg.: Multnomah Books, Questar, 1993.

Notes

1. Deborah S. David and Robert Brannon, eds., *The Forty-Nine Percent Majority* (Reading, Mass.: Addison-Wesley, 1976), 13-36; quotation, 35-36.

2. Richard P. Olson, *Changing Male Roles in Today's World: A Christian Perspective for Men—and Women Who Care about Them* (Valley Forge, Pa.: Judson Press, 1982), 18-24.

3. Cited in David D. Gilmore, *Manhood in the Making: Cultural Concepts of Masculinity* (New Haven: Yale University Press, 1990), 22.

4. Gilmore, *Manhood in the Making*, 220.

5. Ibid., 17.

6. Ibid., 173.

7. Ibid., 11.

8. Ibid., 221.

9. Cited ibid., 146.

10. Cited ibid., 19.

11. Gilmore, *Manhood in the Making*, 229.

12. Ibid., 202-9.

13. Ibid., 211.

14. Ibid., 209-26.

15. Ibid., 230.

16. Ibid., 230-31.

17. Robert Moore and Douglas Gillette, *King, Warrior, Magician, Lover* (San Francisco: Harper, 1990), 9.

18. Jack Balswick, *Men at the Crossroads: Beyond Traditional Roles and Modern Options* (Downers Grove, Ill.: InterVarsity Press, 1992), 43.

19. Moore and Gillette, *King, Warrior, Magician, Lover,* 82.

20. Stu Weber, *Tender Warrior: God's Intention for a Man* (Sisters, Oreg.: Multnomah Books, Questar, 1993); Aaron R. Kipnis, *Knights without Armor: A Practical Guide for Men in Quest of Masculine Soul* (New York: Jeremy P. Tarcher/Putnam Book, G. P. Putnam's Sons, 1991).

21. Kipnis, *Knights without Armor,* 136.

22. Ibid., 142.

23. Christopher X. Burant, "Of Wild Men and Warriors," in *Wingspan: Inside the Men's Movement,* ed. Christopher Harding (New York: St. Martin's Press, 1992), 175.

24. Aaron R. Kipnis, "The Blessings of the Green Man," in *Wingspan,* ed. Harding, 62-67.

25. Balswick, *Men at the Crossroads,* 47.

26. Moore and Gillette, *King, Warrior, Magician, Lover,* 124-25.

27. Van Gennep, cited in Gilmore, *Manhood in the Making,* 124-25.

28. Bly, cited in Frank Pittman III, *Man Enough* (New York: G. P. Putnam's Sons, 1993), 135.

29. Moore and Gillette, *King, Warrior, Magician, Lover,* 6.

30. Gilmore, *Manhood in the Making,* viii.

31. Balswick, *Men at the Crossroads,* 53.

32. Patrick Arnold, cited in Burant, "Of Wild Men and Warriors," in *Wingspan,* ed. Harding, 175.

3

Feelings

"What's the big deal about emotions?"

I found the answer to my question the hard way!

Along with many others, I had noted a tremendous difference in the ways males and females lived their emotional lives. (I refer to trends and averages, although exceptions certainly exist among both males and females.) I once heard a comedian describe it this way. Women, he said, are like a high-tech satellite dish, capable of receiving hundreds of stations. Sensitively and precisely, they discern and sort out a wide range of emotional signals. On the other hand, men are like a "rabbit-ear" antenna with a few pieces of foil hanging from it. They receive just a few stations, and those in a visual "snowstorm"!

Women indeed often seem to have a wider range of feelings and greater freedom to express emotions than do men. They also often have the ability to make distinctions between similar emotions and pinpoint what they are feeling. Further, frequently they detect what is going on emotionally in a person or a group before anything is spoken. Many women feel free to discuss the feelings they discover and to ask for help in dealing with them. It is a topic they find interesting, even fascinating.

On the other hand, men seem to recognize a smaller range of emotions and to express them even less. Even when they feel things deeply, they may have difficulty showing it. They may think, for whatever reason, that they need to keep a tight control on emotions—especially certain ones. They may not recognize these inner messages, or they simply may not feel the need to express their emotions very often.

I had observed and experienced all this. My question was, "So what? Does it really matter that men and women 'do emotions' differently? Isn't it OK if men less frequently recognize emotions, experience emotions, express emotions?"

As I said, I received an answer to my question, but it came the hard way. A few months ago I went in for what I thought was a routine physical exam. When I mentioned a vague occasional pain in my upper chest, my physician took immediate action. At once he administered a cardiogram and then a treadmill test. When I had been on the treadmill for only a few minutes, I heard him say, "Textbook case!" That's not something you want your doctor to say at such a time!

Before the week was out, I had undergone (1) a heart catheterization, which revealed a 95 percent blockage in my "descending anterior artery"; (2) an angioplasty procedure (opening of the constricted passage by means of an inflatable balloon guided from my groin up to my heart); (3) the insertion of a "stent," a spring that increases the chances of keeping that vessel open; and (4) several days of complete bed rest. My physician told me that before these procedures were developed, such a blockage was known as the "widow maker"!

While I was still in the hospital, a nurse stopped by and invited me to participate in cardiac rehabilitation classes, which I began a few weeks later.[1] These classes included a carefully monitored exercise program along with a series of presentations about the nature of my illness—cardiovascular disease—and the ways of managing it. I learned that cardiovascular disease is the hardening and constriction of blood vessels that can lead to heart attack and stroke. It is a progressive illness, but its progress can be slowed and even possibly reversed. If a person does not take certain steps, other "heart incidents" will almost surely follow.

This statement grabbed my attention, and I wanted to take those life-preserving steps—all lifestyle changes, easy to name but difficult to maintain. The disease can be retarded—and possibly reversed—by weight loss, a low-fat diet, exercise, and stress management. Each of the risk factors can cause a problem by itself. Some have suffered heart attacks just because of stress, including unrecognized and unexpressed emotions, in their lives.

And so I did indeed receive an answer to my question the hard way. The title of one book on stress management puts it vividly: *Is It Worth Dying For?*

I am deeply grateful for modern medical technology and the skilled people who opened the blood vessel to my heart. Now it is up to me to keep it open! One of the ways I will do this is by a new method of dealing with my stress and emotions.

What Will We Gain?

There is great benefit in developing a freer emotional life.

1. I gain a better chance at having a long and healthy life.

Although the story I told was scary for me, it is a common one in today's world. Nutritionist David Meinz puts it this way. If you have visited the Vietnam War Memorial in Washington, D.C., you have seen the list of the 57,000 people who died in that long, drawn-out war. The nation properly grieves the loss of those lives. However, the same number of Americans (57,000) die of heart disease every six weeks![2] And the vast majority of them are men.

A similar story can be told about cancer. (Cardiovascular disease and cancer are the two biggest killers in the United States, robbing many people of the opportunity they would otherwise have for a long life.) Research has revealed a connection between unresolved emotions and the onset of cancer. It has also revealed the healing impact of healthy emotions and positive imaging. Emotions have a biological impact on my body, either contributing to its healing or damaging it. Stress management including emotional wisdom greatly improves my chances of a long and healthy life.

2. I improve my relationships with people who are important to me.

If I am under stress and overextended emotionally without recognizing it, I may do things that damage my place in the world. I may do things to the extreme, like drinking, gambling, spending. I may avoid things I would normally do, like play with my children or take my share of the work at the office. I may become edgy or irritated, angry or hostile, bitter or cynical. In my frustration, I may even lapse into abusive behavior, verbal or physical.

On the other hand, if I am in touch with the pressures and my feelings, I can do much to enrich relationships. I can face conflicts rather than run away from them. And when I face conflict, I will have a broader range of options than rage and violence. I can recognize when something is my problem and not take it out on someone else. I can express appreciation, warmth, love, and support. I can ask for help with the feelings or problems that are too great for me to handle alone. *Being in touch with my feelings and expressing them appropriately to others builds community and helps resolve problems.*

3. I enjoy life more.

It has been noted that the only feeling many men feel free to express is sexual feeling. That is too bad, because there is such a wide range of emotions to be experienced. A man may miss those others and place far too heavy a burden on his sex life—which may not be very good or may be nonexistent. Then he has no place to express his emotions.

When we live using only our thoughts, suppressing our emotions, life is like a black-and-white picture. Life that adds emotions to thought is like a many-colored, delicately shaded picture. It embraces so much more of what there is to see, experience, and enjoy.

Appreciation of beauty, joyfulness, love, sadness, laughter (yes, especially laughter), protectiveness, neediness—how much richer life is if I can recognize these emotions in myself and express them out loud (or in some other way). When one is in touch with a variety of emotions, some pressure is taken off one's sex life. And even the sexual expression may improve.

We males may not need the entire repertoire of emotions many females have. But we do need a greater openness to our basic feelings and greater freedom to express them. By gaining in this area we both save and enrich our lives.

4. I experience greater richness in my spiritual life and growth.

Just as emotional wisdom is related to my physical well-being, so it is related to my spiritual well-being. Emotional freedom is not identical to spiritual growth, but it is closely related. By being freer emotionally, I open the door to being freer spiritually. I also am able to experience more dimensions in my spiritual life. We will explore this in greater detail later in this chapter.

Why Is Emotional Expression So Difficult for Us Males?

To recognize the truth that males find emotional expression difficult is a long way from acting on this truth. It is extremely difficult to gain greater freedom with emotions. Many explanations for why this is so have been offered. Some say that for centuries males haven't expressed much emotion because of their role in the workplace. In the early days of history, when food was obtained by hunting, men were often the hunters. Hunting required that one suppress fear, face danger, and perhaps sacrifice oneself for the common good. In later times—say, in the feudal estate or during the industrial revolution or in the era of the modern corporation—many men would confess that they don't enjoy their work or the way they are treated in the workplace. Because of the responsibility of providing for their families, however, they swallow these emotions and plod on.

Others say that our culture has glorified the silent, unexpressive, independent man—the cowboy, the pioneer, the explorer. The Lone Ranger, the protagonist in *The Old Man and the Sea*, movie stars like John Wayne—all these are examples of unexpressed, restrained emotion. And they are held up as some sort of ideal. As John Hough and Marshall Hardy observe in their book, "One of the most prominent ideals in our culture is that men are supposed to be strong enough, competent enough and intelligent enough to handle their problems on their own. Especially emotional problems."[3]

Still others note that males, uncertain of how to express emotions appropriately, look to peers for guidance. But these peers buy into the prevailing norms of male behavior and enforce them ruthlessly. Anyone who does not conform is dismissed as being weak.

Certainly some families have bought into this view, taught it, and enforced it. Many grown men vividly recall a time when a parent, probably a father, ridiculed them for crying, perhaps when they were as young as five or six. Many a boy has resolved never to cry again and has very nearly kept that vow. One man in my cardiac rehabilitation class told us, "I was taught never to cry."

But none of these explanations, however accurate, tells us how we got in this destructive cycle in the first place. The fact is that somehow our whole culture has a constricting view of men's emotions, and this view is hurting us—even killing us. If this teaching was ever good for boys and men, it is not good in this time and place. Yet this view is perpetuated.

Modern-day culture has made a few exceptions. Men who have established their male credentials beyond question—career soldiers and professional athletes—may show some emotion and tenderness. General Arnold Schwartzkopf was once asked, "General, aren't you afraid of the man who would cry?" "No," he answered, "I am afraid of the

man who will not cry." We accept that wisdom from him, but
we don't practice it ourselves.

Further, men who have clearly succeeded may find acceptance as the sensitive, emotionally expressive man. Phil
Donahue and Alan Alda come to mind, and it is good to have
such alternative role models. But theirs does not seem to be
a style easy for the rest of us men to imitate. Clearly, we need
to be free to live in a more healthy way.

A Closer Look

Dr. Robert Eliot points out that in regard to stress management, it is particularly true that our bodies and minds have
not yet adjusted to the changed circumstances in which we
live. He observes that as a human race, we lived in forests
and caves for three million years, on the farm for three
thousand years, and in the factory for three hundred years.
Life as we know it today, with modern technology, has existed
for only fifty years. And even that technology has changed
rapidly in the last few years.

Furthermore, the amount of stimulation, choice, and tension in our lives has increased vastly in the last generation
or so. Researchers note that we experience a thousand times
more events per year than our great-grandparents did. The
time available for decision making about these events has
decreased dramatically.[4]

For millions of years, one's senses needed to be tuned for
the slightest sound that might indicate great physical danger. When our ancestors who lived in the forest heard that
signal of danger, their whole body system immediately went
into stress response. We call it the "fight-or-flight response."
The fight response was one of anger and the urge to confront
the danger. The flight response was one of fear and the urge
to escape the danger. The term "fight or flight" has become
almost a cliché in our day. (Some speak of being "skunks"
[fight] or "turtles" [flight, or at least withdrawal] when
threatened.) The familiarity of the term should not blind us
to the fact that our body systems make responses that
greatly influence our health for good or ill.

For either fight or flight, our ancestors' bodies made a number of extremely useful adaptations. The nervous system released two chemicals into the system, adrenaline and cortisol, which increased strength and energy. Cardiovascular activity increased, providing the blood for increased action; heart rate and blood pressure went up. Muscles shortened and became much stronger. Any bleeding would clot more quickly. The body also mobilized fuels, releasing blood sugar, cholesterol, and fats into the bloodstream. All of these bodily reactions empowered our ancestors to fight strongly or flee swiftly, giving them excellent resources for an emergency.

Today, we rarely experience that drastic physical danger, and yet our bodies *still respond the same way*. Rather than *emergency* stress situations, we now have *chronic* stress situations (and a thousand times more of them than did our great-grandparents). We contend with traffic jams, inconsiderate drivers, rumors about downsizing at our place of work, tensions with friends or spouses or children. Dr. Eliot notes, "As a result, you end up pumping high-energy chemicals (those needed for fighting or fleeing) for low-energy needs." He sums up: "In the twentieth century, the fight-or-flight response is *physiologically neurotic.*"[5]

Indeed it is. In a huge emergency, the body uses the chemicals in responding. With our series of small crises—chronic stress, if you will—the body does not use these chemicals. John-Roger and Peter McWilliams point out that the fight-or-flight response puts enormous physiological stress on the body.

It opens us to diseases (the immune system being told, "Hold off on attacking those germs—we have wild beasts to fight!"), digestive troubles (ulcers and cancers at the far side of it), poor assimilation (preventing necessary proteins, vitamins and minerals from entering the system), slower recovery from illnesses (conquering a disease is far less important than conquering a wild beast), reduced production of blood cells and other necessary cells, sore muscles, fatigue and a general sense of ick, blah, and ugh.

Sound bad? It gets worse.

The emergency chemicals, unused, eventually begin breaking down into other, more toxic substances. Our body must then mobilize—yet again—to get rid of the poisons. The muscles stay tense for a long time after the Response is triggered, especially around the stomach, chest, lower back, neck and shoulders. (Most people have chronic tension in at least one of these areas.) We feel jittery, nervous, uptight.[6]

And these effects in turn can lead to breakdown of blood vessels and the forming of plaque within them, leading to possible heart attack and stroke.

If that isn't bad enough, not only minor crises can stir this reaction, but the mind can invent some crises of its own! Or it worries about a perceived or real problem. Or the mind remembers past minor crises with resentment and anger, each one stirring this emergency stress response again—and again and again.

On rare occasions this stress reaction is a life saver. On repeated occasions, the same stress reaction is a killer. In both circumstances, the response is triggered by those two most basic of all emotions—fear and anger.

Our world, our health, our own welfare and that of those we love, call out to us to find a better way to manage those emotional responses to the stress that is always present.

What about Those Feelings?

It is important for us to recognize stressful situations and the feelings that these stir within us. And experiencing and managing those emotions is essential to our health. How are men doing in this regard? The answer on the whole, unfortunately, is "Not very well"!

In *The Hazards of Being Male,* Herb Goldberg accurately describes our dilemma. He titles his chapter on this subject "Feelings: The Real Male Terror." When he was asked what needs or impulses or emotions males are blocking, he answered, "More or less all of them."

Goldberg notes, "there is still great discomfort and embarrassment when a man overtly and spontaneously expresses his emotions, breaks down in tears, rages in open anger or hate, trembles and shakes in fear, or even laughs too boisterously."[7] Though he wrote those words twenty years ago, present-day counselors echo the same observation. Gary Oliver, writing in the 1990s, explores this identical issue in his book *Real Men Have Feelings Too*. He tells of asking men about their emotions. Here are some of the answers he received: "Emotions are like a foreign language to me." "Emotions are what women have." "I rarely feel any emotions"—except perhaps at a sporting event.[8] For all the positive changes in men, still they lack inner freedom and outer encouragement to deal with feelings very openly. Let's take a look at some of the feelings where difficulties are experienced.

Fear

As we said, one of the basic stress responses is flight-fear. This is one that we must relearn and redirect in these days of constant stress. And yet an honest recognition and admission of fear is hard to come by, for a man. Goldberg writes, "Words like 'chicken-sh__,' 'scaredy cat,' 'coward,' 'gutless,' 'no balls,' and 'sissy' ring in the male's ears a lifetime and often drive him into senseless, self-destructive, even crazy behaviors and risk-taking in order to prove to himself and others, over and over again, that he is a man and that he isn't afraid."[9]

Not only is it hard for a man to admit to himself that he is afraid, it is hard for those around him to accept this. After all, they depend on him, and if he is afraid, what hope is there for them? A friend of mine, a feminist, said of her husband, "I don't mind if he cries once in a while, but I'd feel very uncomfortable if he were afraid."

A man's greatest fear may be that of failing—not being able to care for and provide for those to whom he is committed. And of all his fears, that is the one above all that others around him don't want to hear—it shakes them too much.

I understand this dilemma from my own life. Sometimes I've been told, "Dick, you're a rock." I suppose that means that these friends experience me as fearless or faithful, reliable, caring, genuine, enduring. For the most part that feels good—whenever possible, that's what I want to be for my friends, congregation, and counseling clients. But I too am mortal, fragile, and frail—I discovered that with force as I lay on a hospital bed waiting for my heart procedure. At such a time, I needed to live with my feelings and be in touch with my own mortality. I needed to be allowed my fear, so that my strength would eventually reappear. This could happen only when I recognized and admitted my fear, lived with the risks, and took all the steps I could to reduce those risks.

Anger and Conflict

A man's dilemma concerning anger, the other basic stress response, is somewhat different. Although anger is an emotion associated with men, its expression is curiously limited. It is expected, for the most part, that a man's anger and aggression will be expressed impersonally. That is, he will express it toward strangers, competitors, opponents, or other outside targets.

To put it another way, a male is guided to displace his anger and aggression away from the persons with whom he regularly interacts—probably the people with whom the conflicts, frustrations, and misunderstandings occurred. He is to direct his anger impersonally, toward those with whom he has very little contact.

Let's step back from this dilemma for a moment and think about what anger can mean in a person's life. Anger is often a spontaneous hint or clue that something is wrong. As Gary Oliver puts it, "Anger is to our lives like a smoke detector is to a house, like a dash warning light is to a car, and like a flashing yellow light is to a driver."[10] In *The Dance of Anger,* Harriet Lerner writes,

> Anger is a signal and one worth listening to. Our anger may be a message that we are being hurt, that our rights

are being violated, that our needs or wants are not being adequately met, or simply that something is not right. Our anger may tell us that we are not addressing an important emotional issue in our lives, or that too much of our self—our beliefs, values, desires, or ambitions—is being compromised in a relationship. . . . Just as physical pain tells us to take our hand off the hot stove, the pain of our anger preserves the very integrity of our self.[11]

However, if we barely acknowledge our anger, direct it at impersonal outside forces, and suppress it, we are unintentionally sending our body many strong stress signals. As we noted above, our body responds to these with an "all points alert" activation of many body systems.

Gilda Carle, a communications specialist, warns, "Anger that isn't accepted and confronted openly can be lethal. It leads to stress, burnout and physical illness."[12]

Charles Cole, a psychologist at Colorado State University, points out that the person who stays angry and hostile long after the event that occasioned the anger may be committing slow suicide. He studied the reactions to stress and anger in more than eight hundred patients. His findings confirm what we have earlier noted. The physiological effects of mismanagement of anger and other emotions may cause blood vessels to constrict, increase heart rate and blood pressure, and eventually lead to the destruction of heart muscle. He concludes, "We don't have a thought that doesn't have a physiological consequence."[13]

Other Emotions

There are many other emotions that we males have come to ignore, not feel, repulse, or deny.

We find it hard to admit being dependent or needy, even when we are. Many of us have a hard time accepting that we are sick. Even more, we have a hard time taking the time that skilled medical practitioners recommend to recover from surgery or illness. This is so difficult for us men! After my recent heart procedure, one of my daughters chided me for telling my congregation (in essence), "I am not as sick as you think I am. I can do anything I could do before my hospitalization."

We have a hard time admitting to being tired or worn out, or even that we are sleeping—at least *I* do. I have a phone by my bed, and occasionally I receive an emergency call in the middle of the night. Groping for the phone out of a sound sleep, I automatically deny it if the caller asks me if I was sleeping!

We find it hard to admit we can't handle something on our own and need help. "I can do it by myself. I don't need any help. The Lord helps those who help themselves." Those are more frequent slogans among males than "I can't manage this alone. Can you help me?"

We have a hard time with sadness and tears. Once when leading a men's group, I told a story of a man who broke down and cried at work; I then asked the group if any ever had or ever would cry at work. I expected their response but was surprised at the intensity. One man said, "My boss instructs us, 'Leave your emotions at the door.'" Another answered, "I've cried about work, but never at work. I longed for that kind of rapport, but it was just never there." Still another responded, "Where I work, even if I received word of a death in my family, I would show no outward expression. Certainly I would not cry."

We also have a hard time with love, tenderness, empathy, sympathy. A story is told of an old Scandinavian couple. The husband reached over, patted his wife on the hand, and said, "You mean so much to me that some days it's all I can do to keep from telling you!"

I once attended a workshop led by the late pioneering family therapist Virginia Satir. She worked with a family (father, mother, two foster teenage sons) and asked each in turn, "What's your language for saying 'I love you'?" Each of the males responded by saying he would either *do something* extra, or *buy something*. Expressing tenderness by doing is OK if both sender and receiver understand the message. However, we have a better chance of sharing the benefits of these most enjoyable emotions if we have a wider repertoire for expressing them. It is good to seek for verbal, visual, kinesthetic (involving touch), and action-based ways of expressing love.

Depression is another emotional state that men have difficulty recognizing and expressing. Psychologists have termed depression "the common cold of mental illness" because it is so widespread. And yet men may contend with a long-term low-grade depression and not know it because they have rarely experienced anything else.

Silliness, clowning, playfulness, uninhibited laughter are not thought of as appropriate behaviors for men either—at least not for "sober" men. Think about that word. It's only OK to be happy if you're drunk, it seems!

Steps toward Wholeness

What, then, can we do to manage stress effectively and be in better touch with our emotions?

1. *Find a safe place.*

First, we find a safe place or, more accurately, safe places where we can explore our emotions and the self-talk we've been carrying on about them, whether we knew it or not. Clearly, we won't do this if everything feels fine. However, if our body gives us messages that all is not well, if life is seeming empty, if we have lost our zest for living, or if people we care about find us impossible to live with, then we may recognize a need for change and seek help.

But even when we males are feeling bad, we may resist seeking help. I remember a man with whom I had had a friendly relationship for years. For a long time he resisted friends' suggestions that he come to me for counseling. In his words, "I don't want anyone messing with my head."

In truth, counseling is just the opposite from "messing with one's head." Rather, it is helping a person feel free enough inside to listen to his own inner voices, sort them out, and find his own wisdom and true way. The man I mentioned eventually came to me and used me as a resource to make important decisions about the direction of his life.

But men have a hard time reaching out for such help. Their usual slang term for a psychiatrist (or almost any other counselor) is *shrink*. This is an abbreviation for "head shrinker," a reference, I guess, to primitive witch doctors who reputedly shrank the heads of beheaded victims. That's not a lot of trust with which to begin a helping relationship! Add to that men's reluctance to ask for any kind of help, and we have a difficult situation. Clearly many of us men have a need to move into the uncomfortable, to admit a need for change, and to look for the safest place to begin this process.

That safe place may be with a good and trusted friend, particularly one who is a good listener. Even with a long-term friend, you may need to ask for a change in the ways you relate. You may need to ask permission to talk about deep needs, important feelings, memories. Then tell your friend all you remember about what you were taught about emotions, what makes sense and what doesn't. Talk about present situations and present feelings.

That safe place may be with a counselor. If you do not feel comfortable with the first counselor you see, you should feel free to try others. Folks need to "shop" for a good counselor in much the way one shops for a good mechanic or plumber. Ask for recommendations (you may want to ask your doctor and your minister for suggestions). Do a beginning interview. Ask what the person sees ahead in counseling with you. Discuss fees and insurance. See if these services and terms are what you can live with. If not, talk to another. And another and another, if need be.

That safe place may be a men's support group. Quite likely, freedom to talk about these sensitive, unexamined places of one's life will not come quickly. However, in a good men's group one can share stories and experience growing respect, love, and trust. One will be able to compare one's own experiences with those of other men. In time, the chance to share and receive insights will come.

The safe place may be one of the men's gatherings described in chapter 1. For some men, gathering in an outdoor setting, engaging in rituals from other times and places, drumming and chanting together allow them to get in touch with themselves. There one may get distance and perspective, experience and imagine other ways of being, and again receive the wisdom of other men.

The safe place may be a men's therapy group conducted by a skilled mental health professional. For example, in his book *In the Company of Men,* Marvin Allen tells of using "rage releasing" techniques with individual male clients and with his men's therapy groups. When he senses that a man is not in touch with his anger and rage, he offers him a bat and a large pillow. He tells the client to get down on his knees in front of the pillow, pick up the bat, and allow his anger to surface. He encourages the person to make sounds, to talk out loud, scream, or yell if he feels like it, to tell what he is experiencing.[14] He repeatedly uses this technique to help men get in touch with their feelings and raise them to consciousness so that they can deal with them. He notes that often once a man's anger has surfaced, his grief soon follows. A healing process begins. That is one example of what a skillfully led men's therapy group might be able to do to help a man.

The good news is that a man doesn't have to choose among these safe places (and there may well be others). One can turn to friends *and* groups *and* counselors *and* men's gatherings *and* whatever may be of help. Find the safe places.

2. *Learn to recognize and name the stressor and the emotion.*

Robert Fulghum tells of an experience he had when he was a young adult and was working at a summer resort hotel. He was extremely upset because the manager decreed that for their meals, the help—including him—would eat wieners and sauerkraut, three days in a row. And the cost of meals was deducted from his pay! He sounded off about this situation, on and on, to the night accountant. This person had survived Auschwitz, liked his job, liked the solitude (except for the hour he overlapped with Fulghum), liked having something to eat, including wieners and sauerkraut. He listened to Robert's tirade about as long as he could stand it, and then he said, "You know what's wrong with you, Fulghum? You can't distinguish between a problem and an inconvenience."[15] Sauerkraut and wieners for three days is not a problem; it's an inconvenience!

In our next step, we need to become equally accurate in identifying and labeling things. We are attempting a program of reeducation, of informed self-talk. We need to bring the unconscious to consciousness.

Our basic question is "What am I feeling?" That may not be an easy question to answer. Like many others, we may have misused the word *feelings*. Feelings are not thoughts: "I feel the wage scale at your job is below standard." Feelings are not opinions: "I feel they are treating you unfairly." Feelings are not advice: "I feel you should quit and seek employment elsewhere." All those are misuses of the word *feeling*. Feelings are emotions—anger, fear, love, joy, sorrow, hate, and so on.

Getting in touch with feelings will seem strange and uncomfortable. It will require attention and intention. Perhaps you will want to put the question "What am I feeling?" on your bathroom mirror, your refrigerator, your bench or desk at work. If no answers come, make it a little more vague: "What might I be feeling?" Do self-talk on the question. Do what is happening and what I feel seem to be a good match? Am I overreacting, underreacting? Discuss what you find with the persons in your safe place.

In addition to naming the emotion, we need to start listening for the intensity. My fear may range from my being slightly uneasy to being frozen with terror, with many gradations between. My anger may range from mild annoyance to deep raging and vexed hostility. My sadness may be an occasional loneliness, or it may be a feeling of abandonment and desolation. What am I feeling, and how intensely am I feeling it?[16]

Likewise we need to recognize where stress is occurring in our lives. Make a list of your stress points over the last few days. Mark the ones that were dangerous stress points and which were "chronic," repeated stress points.

Of course, not all stress is harmful. In fact, we would have rather dull lives without some stress. But we need to be sure that the stress is manageable and that we have ways to relieve the stress when it feels like too much.

3. *Be reasonable.*

We need to be reasonable about our emotions, or perhaps we need a new way to understand our emotions. The ways we react emotionally are largely learned responses. We live life the way we do because we were so taught. The persons who taught us may have done their teaching intentionally, believing they had chosen the best course for us. Or they may have automatically and unthinkingly taught us what they were taught.

An important alternative school of thought known as Rational Emotive Therapy can give us some insights and methods here. Its basic premise is that "your emotions are largely determined by how you think and talk to yourself. In other words, *you—not something or someone outside you— play the most important role in determining what you feel* [or don't feel]."[17] Again, it is good to have a counselor and friends listen in on our reflections on emotions. This method can help us males recognize where we have "reasonable" emotions. It can also help us discover faulty thinking about emotions and better ways of living with these feelings.

The advocates of Rational Emotive Therapy point out how thinking influences feeling in an A-B-C fashion:

A is an *Activating Event* that draws one's attention. It may be something external or something internal. For example, I am waiting for a friend with whom I will have dinner, and the friend is late.

B is the *Belief* I have about the meaning of the event, my interpretation of it. This takes the form of "self-talk," a sort of conversation with myself that may be accurate or not, constructive or destructive. My self-talk may become irrational if I base it on long-standing habitual beliefs that I have not reexamined. For example, I may have been taught as a child never to be late, that it is always rude and inconsiderate to be late.

C points to the *Consequences* of A and B. These consequences can take three forms—feelings, physical
reactions, and behaviors.

I will probably add a great deal of stress to a situation that
already has a moderate amount if I bring irrational, negative
self-talk to it. The stress may be even worse if I jump from the
situation (A) to a feeling, behavior, or symptom (C) without
even having an evaluative, thoughtful self-talk (B).[18]
We may need to relearn to express feelings in appropriate
ways. This will require informed self-talk, helped by the
insights and contributions of others. In a workbook on stress
management titled *Becoming Thick-Skinned*, Hermann
Witte identifies a series of irrational self-talks that contribute to unnecessary stress. I mention a few here and offer
suggestions for more informed self-talk in these situations:

a. "Things upset me." The assumption here is that external events exclusively determine how one reacts. One thus
becomes the helpless victim of one's feelings. A more rational
self-talk is "I upset me." I am responsible for my feelings, my
behavior, my interpretations.

b. "I have no control over the nature, intensity, and duration of my emotional responses." (Males have a corollary: "I
have no control over the absence of my emotional responses.") Either way, persons can anticipate stressful
events where possible and make every attempt to respond in
proportion to the stimulus. When surprise events come upon
one, one can carry on realistic conversations with oneself. A
wiser self-talk may be "I may not be able to control getting
upset [or my usual lack of conscious emotional response], but
I have significant control over the intensity and duration of
my feelings."

c. "My emotional and stress responses are inherited." A
parallel belief may also be at work: "My emotional responses
are inherent in being female or being male." This may be one
of the most destructive self-talks of all. Emotional responses
are *human,* not male or female. All of us have grown and
changed in our emotional reactions from infancy to the present. It is so important that we replace this message with a

correcting rational self-talk: "My feelings and behaviors are learned, and if they're ineffective, they can be unlearned." One of my readers, the stepfather of children who have attention deficit disorder (ADD), took strong exception to the idea that statement (c) was irrational and that the suggested self-talk was an improvement. He pointed out that as many as one in ten persons suffer from ADD, oppositional defiant disorder (ODD), Tourette's syndrome, or a kindred disorder. There is strong evidence for inherited predispositions to these conditions. Further, these conditions are sometimes associated with complications like depression and alcoholism. Often a necessary first step is prescribed medication that reduces the tendency to the behavior. Then, perhaps, other guidance, coaching, and counseling can help. This parent pointed out that persons with attention deficit disorder or similar conditions do not improve by being told to "think about what is happening, and choose a better way." As a matter of fact, being told such a thing may increase the guilt, frustration, and problem behavior. Rather, diagnosis and, quite likely, medication will be needed before the person with this disorder can engage in more constructive behavior.[19] The same qualifiers may apply to other self-talk statements as well. I accept this reader's reservations for those contending with this family of conditions. At the same time, for at least nine out of ten people, the insights of Rational Emotive Therapy are likely to serve well.

d. "I can't change the way I react." One's growth and development to this point in life disprove this self-talk. Further, learning to carry on these inner conversations, along with the presence of supportive and wise persons, can further enhance one's growth. The realistic self-talk here is "I can change my emotional responses to stress through realistic, constructive self-talk."[20] Awareness, education, support, and practice can all contribute to this change. Many other destructive self-talks are carried on, but these will serve as starters.

4. *Develop methods to deal with stress and its accompanying emotions.*

If we have put a support system in place, have started to recognize stress and emotions, have begun to reflect on and learn about the emotions in our lives, we still have work to do. We need to learn and practice those things that express emotions and relieve stress reaction for us in healthy ways.
a. Become aware of stressors and emotions.
Anticipate and reduce stressors whenever possible. For example, if I find myself getting upset in traffic, I can plan ahead to give myself more time for travel. Or, as much as possible, I can plan to do my activities outside the rush hours of the day. If I find myself stressed by too much to do in too little time, I can learn to say "no." This may lead to my doing fewer things but doing them better. If I become aware that certain people or certain attitudes—complaining, for example—are irritating to me, I can choose to reduce my associations with such folks as much as possible. Or I can learn to recognize the behavior and refuse to get hooked or engaged by it. The point is that I can apply a thoughtful, self-caring strategy to this aspect of my life. I cannot eliminate stress from my life, nor would I want to. However, by being intentional, I can reduce it to manageable proportions.
b. Learn to give internal self-messages.
In particular, I need to learn to give myself two messages: (1) This is a small crisis, not a big one, a "chronic one" rather than an "emergency one"; (2) This crisis is over, and I can get back to normal. I use the first message, for example, when I am facing traffic pressures. My work involves a fair amount of driving around a city to visit folks in hospitals. Sometimes I can choose the time to go, and at other times I have no control over when I need to be at a hospital. I have found a few things that can keep me from being overstressed while driving. For one, I enjoy both music and talking tapes, so I keep a supply of both in my car at all times. I think of the car time as an opportunity to become refreshed so that I can enter helpfully into whatever crisis folks are having at the hospital. Further, I am fortunate to live in a beautiful city. Even when rushed, I try to remember this and enjoy the beauty of the changing seasons as I drive from place to place.

I think of alternate routes that may provide more scenic views. The other side of this work-related stress is its "hurry up and wait" aspect. I may be rushing to keep a schedule of visiting several hospitals and then arrive at a hospital to learn that my patient is having an X-ray or a physical therapy session and that I have a wait of up to an hour. I can stew and get upset (giving myself those "major crisis" signals), or I can be more creative. I can choose to take a nice brisk walk around the hospital grounds or through the neighborhood (I need aerobic exercise anyway). I can pray and meditate in the hospital chapel. Or I can enjoy a refreshing beverage in the cafeteria.

I may discover that, in the light of this delay, I won't be able to cover all the territory I had hoped, so I can spend a little of the time making phone calls to the less urgently ill persons on my calling list and other calls to rearrange my schedule. I'm still learning, but I am trying to identify little crises as such and manage them accordingly. Think about the "small crises" that occur in your work and life and strategize ways that you can keep them in perspective.

The other skill (2) is to let our body system know that the crisis, whether large or small, is over. Earlier we noted a number of responses our body made to stress. In fact, we can control a few of those body responses and give messages to the rest of our body. These messages can be quite simple. Text books on stress management refer to them as "relaxation exercises."

For example, we noted that under stress, the muscles contract. A relaxation exercise is simply to stretch the muscles. If you are in a private place where you can do so, stand and stretch your muscles by reaching as high as you can and as wide as you can. If you are in a crowded office, stretch as much as you can without drawing undue attention. Another exercise one can do is to tense each set of muscles and then relax them—head, neck, shoulders, arms, torso, legs.

Again, when one is under stress, breathing changes. So one can do conscious breathing exercises. Take deep breaths, breathing as deeply as one can, holding the breaths. In so doing, you slow down breathing. These two techniques—stretching and breathing—can be combined. Breathe in deeply as you stand and reach as high as you can. Hold the breath for several counts. Then breathe out deeply as you lower your hands. Repeat this three or four times and note the change in your body relaxation. The stress management textbooks listed at the end of this chapter provide a number of helpful relaxation techniques.

c. Use up the energy created by the stress.

My body may have received—accurately or inaccurately—a "major alert" signal and geared itself up for a significant fight-or-flight response. If so, I am wise to find a way to use that accumulated energy. Aerobic exercise, which is a good health practice for more reasons than one, may be the major means of discharging this energy. Running, jogging, or walking; swimming laps; working out with a punching bag; skipping rope; playing a lively game of basketball or tennis; dancing; mowing the lawn—all these provide means of releasing energy and tension so that the body can relax. Our ancestors had more physical ways to relieve stress because they used their bodies in gathering food and fuel. We will probably have to invent our own ways.

None of what I have described here is new, but we can be wiser and more intentional in using these methods to make stress more manageable in our lives.

5. *Take hold more firmly of your deep gladness, your true peace.*

Prayer and meditation can provide powerful resources and strength in dealing with stress. Some twenty years ago, Herbert Benson, a professor at Harvard Medical School, detailed and measured the good effect of meditation, which he called "the Relaxation Response." He detailed in the simplest language how to meditate and then carefully measured its effect on such stress responses as elevated blood pressure and cardiovascular disease. His scientific tests verified that meditation was indeed a valuable resource for reducing ill effects and increasing health.

As Benson taught it, only four elements were necessary: (1) a quiet environment; (2) a "mental device" such as a word or phrase to repeat; (3) the adoption of a passive, open attitude; and (4) a comfortable position—but not one in which a person would fall asleep. He offered these points not as an innovation but simply as a scientific validation of age-old wisdom common to many religions and cultures. These are the instructions given to folks as they begin learning the relaxation response:

(1) Sit quietly in a comfortable position.

(2) Close your eyes.

(3) Deeply relax all your muscles, beginning at your feet and progressing up to your face. Keep them relaxed.

(4) Breathe through your nose. Become aware of your breathing. As you breathe out, say the word, "ONE," silently to yourself. For example, breathe IN . . . OUT, "ONE"; IN . . . OUT, "ONE"; etc. Breathe easily and naturally.

(5) Continue for 10 to 20 minutes. You may open your eyes to check time, but do not use an alarm. When you finish, sit quietly for several minutes, at first with your eyes closed and later with your eyes opened. Do not stand up for a few minutes.

(6) Do not worry about whether you are successful in achieving a deep level of relaxation. Maintain a passive attitude and permit relaxation to occur at its own pace. When distracting thoughts occur, try to ignore them by not dwelling upon them and return to repeating "ONE." . . . Practice the technique once or twice daily, but not within two hours after any meal, since the digestive processes seem to interfere with the elicitation of the Relaxation Response.[21]

Benson later wrote *Beyond the Relaxation Response,* incorporating into his techniques what he termed the "faith factor"—"one's deepest personal beliefs . . . a deeply held set of philosophical or religious convictions."[22]

The techniques described by Benson should not surprise those of us who embrace the Christian faith. We may recognize that meditation or "the relaxation response" slows down a person and lets a soul be in touch with God whether the person recognizes God (or even believes in God).

And so we need to learn not only to meditate but to pray. We need to do this for many reasons. Managing our stress and emotions in a more healthy fashion is only one of those reasons.

The prayer, however, should not be rote repetition. It should not be hurried, nor should it be a one-way monologue to God. Prayer needs to be something more. Someone once defined prayer as "the time exposure of the soul to God." Another suggested that prayer is meant to be a two-way conversation with God. Another suggested that prayer is "letting go and letting God."

Such prayer may begin with meditation. However, one uses a specific word of one's faith rather than "ONE" (although that can be a helpful word for meditation as well). A word or phrase (sometimes called a mantra) focuses one's attention. There are many possible prayer mantras—God, praise God, Jesus, Friend, Love, Joy, Peace. As Benson suggests, you may repeat the word or phrase each time you breathe. Interrupting thoughts will float in—let them come, and then dismiss them.

Then bring before God's presence any problems, questions, persons with whom you are having problems, persons you hold dear, causes dear to your heart and to God's. Do not rush. It may be that your answer is to feel less tension over your concerns. Perhaps it will be that you see these issues more from God's perspective—seeing the forest rather than the trees. Or it may be that God will speak to you in the depths of your prayer with guidance and wisdom. Or it may be that God is silent on what you ask, for a time.[23]

By all means, be frank and open with God about what you are feeling in the pressures and tensions you lift up to God. God knows us completely, and we need not pretend. It is foolish to be a polite stranger with God. It may well be in our praying that our anguish is turned to peace, our tears into comfort and acceptance, our pain into joy, our anger into serenity.

I have been pointing to a direct connection between the emotions of stress and our physical well-being. But there is also a direct connection between our emotions and our spiritual well-being. Men who aspire to spiritual growth without a greater freedom in emotions will miss some vital aspects of that spiritual journey. Men who seek God's presence in their lives but not in their emotions and times of stress are shutting God out from a most important area.

So, in our reaching for emotional health and strength, we should seek the One who is our true peace and our deep gladness. Do so by finding the style and methods of meditation and prayer that fit you.

6. *Come to grips with your own denial and resistance.*

In this chapter I have shared important life-giving information summarized from many people wise in the art of living. And yet most of this will go right by us males unless we do two things: admit our own denial and come to grips with our own resistance.

Our denial may take this form: "All this stuff about expressing feelings and living with stress may be fine for others, but I don't need it." Or our denial may be, "It's too bad about those other men who can't release their emotions. I'm glad that I'm so good at it."

The latter was my denial. I am a pastoral counselor. I thought I understood about feelings and was doing fine with my own emotions. I have a readily available box of tissues in my office and often offer it to a crying counselee. I encourage a full expression of feelings.

Getting things off your chest—catharsis—and then feeling relief and gaining insight are parts of a very rewarding process. This is true both for my clients and for me. I have felt myself to be unshockable, willing to be at the side of my clients to face any problem, behavior, crisis, or tragedy they might experience.

All that was, and is, true—and yet . . . I was not as good a counselor to myself as I was to others. I thought I was doing fine with my emotions and stress management—until it hit me in my left anterior descending artery and almost killed me. I can still deny, or I can face the connection between my stress and emotions and my body, my health, my spiritual life. Then maybe I can do something about it.

That does mean unlearning some lifetime habits and learning some new ones. The process is uncomfortable. I learn slowly and change even more slowly. This discomfort might be called resistance. At this point I recall the advice of one of my counseling supervisors. He said, "Respect the resistance you find in your counselees. But push on it. It is at those points of resistance that there is the greatest opportunity for growth."

Since my heart incident, I have been eating a low-fat diet, losing weight, and engaging in aerobic exercise at least three times a week. I am slowly learning to do more stress management and self-talk about *my* emotions and pressures. Because of these practices in response to my crisis, I am the healthiest I have been in years. A life of deep joy, emotional aliveness, and deepened relationships beckons to me, if only I face my denials and continue to push on my resistances.

You alone can decide where my story touches yours. My hope for you is that you choose life—full, rich, and free.

Invitations

Here are some areas of growth or discovery that you may want to explore:

__ Make an appointment you have been postponing, perhaps for a long-delayed "annual physical" with your physician, perhaps with your pastor, perhaps with a counselor.

__ Talk with a close friend about feelings—the ones that come easily, the ones that you have difficulty expressing.

__ Take a stress management course (they are often offered by hospitals).

__ Make plans for a systematic exercise program. Do the enrolling, make the connections, or purchase the equipment that will get you going.

___ Take steps to deepen your prayer and meditation life. Perhaps you need a prayer partner or a spiritual guide.

___ Write your own:

_____

_____

Questions for Conversation and Group Discussion

1. Reflect on your early experiences with emotions. Were you encouraged to experience and express all your emotions? If you had sisters, were you socialized differently regarding emotions?

2. Make a list of the times of stress in your life in the last month. Compare them with at least one other person. What were the wisest things you did to manage that stress? What could you have done that would have been easier on you?

3. Discuss the list of emotions the author says are hard for men to express. Is what he says true of you? Or do you feel you have greater freedom than he suggests?

4. Have you ever had a health problem that your physician told you might be related to stress or emotions? What kind of health problem?

5. In your opinion is greater freedom about emotions and spiritual growth connected? If so, in what ways?

6. Have you had experiences where prayer or meditation helped you deal with stress or upset feelings? If so, could you tell another about it?

Resources

Allen, Marvin, with Jo Robinson. *In the Company of Men* (also published under the title *Angry Men, Passive Men*). New York: Random House, 1993.

Benson, Herbert. *Beyond the Relaxation Response*. New York: Berkley Books, 1984.

————. *The Relaxation Response*. New York: William Morrow, 1975.

————. *Timeless Healing*. New York: Scribner's, 1997.

Culbertson, Philip L. *Counseling Men*. Minneapolis: Fortress Press, 1994.

————. *New Adam*. Minneapolis: Fortress Press, 1992.

Eliot, Robert S., and Dennis L. Breo. *Is It Worth Dying For?* New York: Bantam Books, 1984.

Fulghum, Robert. *Uh-Oh*. New York: Villard Books, 1991.

Goldberg, Herb. *The Hazards of Being Male: Surviving the Myth of Masculine Privilege*. New York: Signet Book, New American Library, 1976.

Hough, John, and Marshall Hardy. *Against the Wall: Men's Reality in a Codependent Culture*. Houston: Hazelden Foundation, 1991.

John-Roger and Peter McWilliams. *You Can't Afford the Luxury of a Negative Thought*. Los Angeles: Prelude Press, 1991.

Kirsta, Alix. *The Book of Stress Survival*. New York: Simon and Schuster, 1986.

Lerner, Harriet Goldhor. *The Dance of Anger: A Woman's Guide to Changing the Patterns of Intimate Relationships*. New York: Harper and Row, 1985.

Meinz, David L. *How to Lose Weight and Keep It Off. Fat, Fiber, and FBI*. Undated audiotapes.

Minirth, Frank, and Paul Meier, with Don Hawkins, Chris Tburman, and Richard Flouroy. *The Stress Factor*. Chicago: Northfield Publishing, 1992.

Nadeau, Kathleen G., ed. *A Comprehensive Guide to Attention Deficit Disorder in Adults*. New York: Brunner/Mazel, 1995.

Oliver, Gary J. *Real Men Have Feelings Too*. Chicago: Moody Press, 1993.

Pipkin, H. Wayne. *Christian Meditation: Its Art and Practice*. New York: Hawthorn Books, 1977.

Notes

1. I express my appreciation to that nurse, Terry Chaffee, B.S.N., head of the Cardiac Rehabilitation Unit at Shawnee Mission Medical Center. Terry stimulated and clarified my thinking on this subject, suggested helpful resources, and helpfully critiqued this chapter.

2. David L. Meinz, *How to Lose Weight and Keep It Off*, and *Fat, Fiber, and FBI*, undated audiotapes.

3. John Hough and Marshall Hardy, *Against the Wall: Men's Reality in a Codependent Culture* (Houston: Hazelden Foundation, 1991), 30.

4. Robert S. Eliot and Dennis L. Breo, *Is It Worth Dying For?* (New York: Bantam Books, 1984), 23, 13.

5. Ibid., 24, 23.

6. John-Roger and Peter McWilliams, *You Can't Afford the Luxury of a Negative Thought* (Los Angeles: Prelude Press, 1991), 29-31.

7. Herb Goldberg, *The Hazards of Being Male: Surviving the Myth of Masculine Privilege* (New York: Signet Book, New American Library, 1976), 42.

8. Gary J. Oliver, *Real Men Have Feelings Too* (Chicago: Moody Press, 1993), 59.

9. Goldberg, *Hazards of Being Male,* 48-49.

10. Oliver, *Real Men,* 100.

11. Harriet Goldhor Lerner, *The Dance of Anger: A Woman's Guide to Changing the Patterns of Intimate Relationships* (New York: Harper and Row, 1985), 1.

12. Quoted in Oliver, *Real Men,* 109.

13. Quoted ibid., 110.

14. Marvin Allen with Jo Robinson, *In the Company of Men* (also published under the title *Angry Men, Passive Men*) (New York: Random House, 1993), 130-39.

15. Robert Fulghum, *Uh-Oh* (New York: Villard Books, 1991), 143-46.

16. Oliver, *Real Men,* 67.

17. Eliot and Breo, *Is It Worth Dying For?* 97.

18. Ibid., 97-99.

19. For more information, readers should consult *A Comprehensive Guide to Attention Deficit Disorder in Adults,* ed. Kathleen G. Nadeau (New York: Brunner/Mazel, 1995).

20. Eliot and Breo, *Is It Worth Dying For?* 102-3.

21. Herbert Benson, *The Relaxation Response* (New York: William Morrow, 1975), 159-60.

22. Herbert Benson, *Beyond the Relaxation Response* (New York: Berkley Books, 1984), 5-6.

23. H. Wayne Pipkin, *Christian Meditation: Its Art and Practice* (New York: Hawthorn Books, 1977).

4

Loneliness, Friendships, and Groups

In a "Peanuts" cartoon, Lucy has set up her small booth. It looks like a child's lemonade stand, except for her sign, "Psychiatrist: 5 cents." Charlie Brown comes up to her and asks, "Can you cure loneliness?" Lucy answers, "I can cure anything, Charlie." Charlie persists, "Can you cure deep-down, bottom-of-the-well, black-forever loneliness?" Lucy responds, "All for the same nickel?"

If she could, it would be quite a bargain! The desire to escape from loneliness and to be in the company of good friends is a basic hunger of all of us. A series of immensely popular TV shows has touched upon this longing—*Seinfeld, Friends, Mad about You,* and *Cheers* (with its theme song, "You want to go where everybody knows your name"). In each of these, the characters hang out and spend time with one another. They seem to have the friendships we all desire but don't always have.

In this chapter we will think about loneliness and two ways that men try to escape loneliness—through friendship and groups.

Stories of Great Friendships

Modern TV isn't the only place where friendship is described. Indeed, some of the most stirring stories of friendship are found in the Bible. One of the most beautiful is that of Jonathan and David. In chapter 2 we told the story of David's choosing his own weapons and style in confronting the fearful Goliath and of triumphing in that way. This story begins where that one ends.

After David's victory against Goliath, King Saul and his commander Abner discuss David's success within the hearing of the king's son, Jonathan. They bring David to them and speak with him. In 1 Samuel 18, the story continues: "When David had finished speaking to Saul, the soul of Jonathan was bound to the soul of David, and Jonathan loved him as his own soul. Saul took him that day and would not let him return to his father's house" (vv. 1-2).

Very soon, much of the praise and adulation of the people that has rested on Jonathan and Saul passes to David instead. Jonathan could become very jealous, but he does not. Rather, he offers his admiration and recognition to David as well. Jonathan's soul is knit to the soul of David, and they sense between them a deep bond of brotherhood. Jonathan so loves David that he makes specific promises and gives gifts to express and seal that love. The story continues, "Then Jonathan made a covenant with David, because he loved him as his own soul. Jonathan stripped himself of the robe that he was wearing, and gave it to David, and his armor, and even his sword and his bow and his belt" (v. 4).

It is a time of war and instability, so this idyllic loving friendship is tested all too soon. David's success as a warrior continues. At a victory celebration the women sing, "Saul has killed his thousands, and David his ten thousands" (v. 7). This song stirs Saul's insecurity and jealousy, which grows and grows.

And so Jonathan finds himself in an impossible situation. His father wants him to go into the "family business"—monarchy—but Jonathan apparently has no desire to be king.

Clearly, he demonstrates a complete lack of competitive spirit when it looks as though David will be king, not he. Further, Jonathan feels an intense loyalty to his father, who is, at least, emotionally ill. Increasingly his father's behavior becomes erratic and irrational, motivated by anger, suspicion, and fear. Less and less is Saul able to lead. But Jonathan remains at Saul's side, commander-in-chief of his father's forces.

Saul and David are on a collision course. The tortured and jealous Saul is sure that David is seeking his throne. Jonathan's position is increasingly untenable. He must do all he can to aid his ailing father. He must do all he can to protect his dearest friend. Two desperately incompatible goals!

And yet Jonathan pulls it off. He never does anything that undermines his father's reign. And yet he intercedes, advocates, even acts as a spy for David's safety. One time he succeeds in convincing Saul that David is Saul's friend. The next time Saul is not convinced. When Jonathan asks that David be excused from the monthly feast, Saul lashes out at him, "You son of a crooked whore, do you think that I can't see that you have chosen the son of Jesse [note that David is nameless here, which is a form of dismissal in the biblical text] to your own shame, and the shame of your mother's nakedness?" (This is Philip Culbertson's translation of 1 Samuel 20:30).[1]

Saul's outburst is an extreme statement of how suspicious society in general and men in particular often are of close male friendships. Clearly, Saul thinks that Jonathan's and David's relationship is sexual—with his use of the words *whore, chosen, shame,* and *nakedness.* Culbertson notes, "Saul is quick to judge, just as our society is quick to judge. When men form close friendships with other men, it is symptomatic of our sexually sick society that so many are quick to jump to conclusions."[2] In doing so we also put down and dismiss the power and significance of intimate friendships between men. Jonathan, the superior in the relationship, is nevertheless vulnerable before David. It is in sharing our vulnerabilities that the deepest connections are made. Jonathan and David have one last secret appointment in which Jonathan must break the sad news that David's life is indeed in danger.

> . . . David rose from beside the stone heap and prostrated himself with his face to the ground. He bowed three times, and they kissed each other, and wept with each other; David wept the more. Then Jonathan said to David, "Go in peace, since both of us have sworn in the name of the Lord, saying, 'The Lord shall be between me and you, and between my descendants and your descendants, forever.'" He got up and left; and Jonathan went into the city. (1 Samuel 20:41-42)

In all likelihood, David and Jonathan never see each other again. Jonathan continues to aid his father, and David lives a fugitive's life. In fact, after some years, David seeks asylum with the Philistines and would have been in the opposing army during the final battle, except that some Philistines do not trust him.

On fateful Mount Gilboa, the Israelite army is defeated by those same Philistines, and Saul and Jonathan are both slain. When David hears of it, he is grief stricken. Second Samuel 1 contains his lament:

> Saul and Jonathan, beloved and lovely!
>   In life and in death they were not divided.
> they were swifter than eagles,
>   they were stronger than lions. . . .
> Jonathan lies slain upon your high places.
> I am distressed for you, my brother Jonathan;
>   greatly beloved were you to me;
>   your love to me was wonderful,
>   passing the love of women.
>   —2 Samuel 1:23, 25-26

David and Jonathan's hugs and kisses and David's lament that Jonathan's love was "wonderful, passing the love of women" have stirred speculation. What sort of relationship did Jonathan and David have? Was there a sexual, romantic component? That is possible. It is also possible, however, that two caring men could have a free and loving relationship with such expression that did not connect to sexual passion. Whatever it was, it had depth and power!

When David became king, he searched for any of Saul's house to whom he might show kindness for Jonathan's sake. Jonathan's lame son, Mephibosheth, was still alive. And so David summoned him, gave back to him all the land of his grandfather Saul, and invited him always to eat at the king's table. It was the last thing he could do for his best friend.

Sometimes friendship costs. Sometimes friendship hurts. The cost of a great friendship is the pain that comes when you lose it. For these reasons, Culbertson calls this story a "text of terror for men." Indeed it contains more pain than we usually realize. And yet most would say that the pain of being misunderstood or of losing a wonderful friend is not too great a price to pay for the joy of having a friend.

Consider yet another Bible story, this one occurring a thousand years or so later.[3] It too is the story of friends. A brief passage in 2 Timothy speaks of friends and the need for them. Paul is in a prison cell in Rome, awaiting the continuation and conclusion of his trial. A number of stories lie behind Paul's words. So let's hear his voice and recall the relationships that led to this moment:

> [Timothy,] Do your best to come to me soon. . . . Only Luke is with me. Get Mark and bring him with you, for he is useful in my ministry. . . . Do your best to come before winter. (2 Timothy 4:9, 11, 21)

In this passage, Paul also speaks of a friend who "deserted me," of another "who did me great harm," and of others who have been sent to care for the Christian work in various places. In his extreme and dire circumstances, Paul deeply wanted a circle of three friends around him.

There was Luke, whom Paul described elsewhere as "the beloved physician." Very probably Luke had been of great help to Paul in dealing with the health problems that plagued him all his life. Luke saw Paul arrested and accompanied him on his journey to Rome for trial. Since a prisoner was allowed only two slaves, Luke may well have enrolled himself as Paul's slave in order to stay near and support him in this dangerous adventure. Probably Luke was Paul's peer. Then there were two younger friends in this inner circle. Timothy first appears in the pages of Scripture as an associate of Paul's at Corinth. We can assume that he had been a bright young convert, one in whom Paul saw great promise. It is safe to assume further that Paul mentored him and then called upon him to serve in a number of ways. Paul refers to him in the greetings of several of his letters and often sends him on missions (for instance, to check on the progress of the new Christians at Thessalonica). He refers to Timothy as brother, as son, as servant of Christ, as person of honor. Here is the son Paul never had, one who had not always succeeded in his efforts but who had never let Paul down.

Mark is the other friend whom Paul wants to see. Timothy is to bring him because "he is useful in my ministry." Or, as one translator put it, "for he can turn his hand to anything . . . for he is a useful man to have about the place." This is surprising, for Mark is a young man who "failed his initiation," so to speak. When Paul and Barnabas set out on what we now call their first missionary journey, they took Mark with them as their helper and assistant. His home had been a center of Christian activity from the beginning in Jerusalem (maybe even the scene of the Last Supper). He was grounded in the things of Christ and seemed destined for greatness. But then, at a crucial point in that journey—on a hard and dangerous road to the central plateau of Asia Minor—apparently Mark's nerve and courage failed him. He gave up, left them, and went home.

Paul took that defection hard. When he and Barnabas were about to set out on another missionary journey, he refused to take Mark with them. Barnabas insisted. They quarreled, and so far as we know, they never worked together again. As William Barclay puts it, "There was a time when Paul had no use for Mark, when he looked on him as a spineless deserter, and when he completely refused to have him on his staff."[4]

We don't know what Mark did to compensate for that defection, nor do we know what Paul did to reach out, accept, forgive, and restore. But we know it happened. Anything is possible! In an earlier letter (Colossians), Mark is at Paul's side, and Paul commends Mark to the Colossian church and asks them to receive him. And now the reunion is complete. In my most severe testing, Paul says, I want Mark with me, for he is so completely useful to me.

There is a silent fourth friend of whom Paul does not speak—Barnabas. Barnabas was an old friend to both Paul and Mark. Indeed, years before, when Paul (then called Saul) had had his vision and conversion experience, when the others in Jerusalem did not believe it and were afraid of him, Barnabas was the one who trusted Paul, introduced him, helped others trust him (Acts 9:27). And later, when the Antioch church was growing and needed more leadership, Barnabas—then the leader of this vigorous congregation—remembered Paul, went to Tarsus, recruited him, trusted him with leadership. As we said, they went on a mission tour together. At the time, Barnabas was clearly the leader. The early references in Acts are to "Barnabas and Paul." Gradually, the gifted, aggressive Paul becomes the more prominent. This does not seem to have been a problem to Barnabas.

On one matter, however, he would not budge: he thought Mark deserved a second chance. Over that, he and Paul broke company, and he took Mark with him to give him a second opportunity to make good. It may well have been that in giving notable service with Barnabas, Mark was able to live down his earlier failure. Barnabas is not mentioned or invited in 2 Timothy—we don't know where he was by this time—but he was present in Paul's being recognized as a Christian leader and in Mark's comeback. Would that each of us had a Barnabas in our life! But back to our story.

At that moment captured by the snapshot in 2 Timothy 4, Paul has one friend with him, Luke, and wants two more,

Timothy and Mark. In addition to their presence, he has two simple requests. He asks them to bring his cloak to ward off the chills of a damp and dark Roman prison cell. Further, he asks for his books, that is, the papyrus rolls (possibly early forms of the Gospels), and for the parchments (possibly such necessary legal documents as his proof of citizenship, or else parts of the Hebrew Scriptures).

Just before the verses I have been examining with you, Paul triumphantly exclaims, "I have fought the good fight, I have finished the race, I have kept the faith. From now on there is reserved for me the crown of righteousness. . ." (vv. 7-8). Paul was the Christian "warrior" par excellence! He had endured that Roman cell and faced his trial and probable execution like a soldier.

And yet Paul is also a "lover," a tender, vulnerable friend who cries out to those nearest him, "I know what you are doing is important, but right now, I need you more. *Come before winter!*"

Why Don't I Have More Friends or Deeper Friendships?

I have told these stories in some detail to show the rich variety of friendships that the Bible describes. Research has revealed how important friendship is. Friends can save your life! A number of research projects now demonstrate that warm and secure relationships can "boost immune functions, improve the quality of life, and lower the risk of dying from cancer, coronary artery disease, and other physical and mental health conditions at any age."[5] With an increasing percentage of single adults in the population, friendship may be an even greater need than in the past. This has led one scholar, Pierre Babin, to predict that "the relationships of the future will be those of friendship and small groups."[6]

One response to these stories and information may be, "I wish I had friendships that were so close and satisfying." And this may lead to yet another response, "Why don't I?" It has been widely and repeatedly acknowledged that close, deep, meaningful friendships between men in our culture are all too rare. Forming such friendships is not something we do very well. Two major reasons are often given for this lack.

First, men are poor at forming friendships with other men because of their homophobia, that is, fear of homosexuality. Actually, this fear may actually be a combination of fears—fears of actual sexual attraction or behavior with another male, of appearing feminine, of being seen as having effeminate affect or behavior. Although these are quite different issues, they relate to the same fear. From early on, boys uncertain of themselves fear the names other boys might put on them (we all have heard a variety of offensive names over the years). Such fear-based name calling does not encourage trustful relationships with other males, which can seem quite risky.

I was once subjected to this sort of ridicule, and I must admit it had a certain sting—even though I was an adult. When I lived in another part of the country, a male friend and I used to meet in a city between our homes every few months. We would spend an evening enjoying ourselves together. On one such night we went to a comedy club and were escorted to a front table. As the comic of the evening sparred with the audience, he singled us out, strongly implying that the only reason two men would be at a comedy club together was if they were a gay couple out on a date! The implication: why on earth would two heterosexual men be out having fun together? The uneasy laughter of the crowd caused a mild discomfort. We are both secure in our heterosexual identity, and so the embarrassment passed quickly. For a male not secure in his sexual identity, such an incident would probably have been even more difficult. But why should two males, whatever their sexual orientation, be subjected to that kind of ridicule? No one else present that night got that treatment. Even now, the incident reminds me of that fear, that barrier to deep communion and fellowship between males.

We need clear assurances that same-gender friendships are normal, natural, important, needful. Indeed, some things one needs in life can be received only from a same-gender friend. Males can identify with another male's embarrassment and can see problems from his perspective. Men can offer another male perspective on romantic dilemmas or can let another man know he is not the only one that has had a particular problem.

Second, men are prevented from forming male friendships because of competition. We see each other as rivals for women, for jobs and for success and promotions at those jobs, for power and prestige among other men, and more. When one is competing with another man, it is difficult to get close enough to be a friend. Some male friendships come from competing together against others—as members of an athletic team, a gang, a military unit. Even then, the competition may get in the way—who's the best competitor, the star of this unit?

Competition sometimes sneaks up on us in our friendships when we do not expect it. I remember a conversation with a dear friend of many years. I was about to leave the community after spending almost ten years there. We had similar interests and professions. He and his family were members of my church, and we shared many activities there. Our wives were friends, we were friends to each other's wives, and our children were friends. We had been there for each other in hard times.

In one of our last conversations before I left, he told me that he felt we were competitors. I was shocked and told him I didn't recognize it. He pointed out that competition—wanting to be highly regarded—had kept him from telling me about the increasingly troubled state of his marriage. In this, he needed a friend. I was one of his best friends but was not close enough to be trusted with (or not close enough to hear) this pain. Competition! A hidden barrier even when I hadn't seen it at the time.

Other thoughts or attitudes can hinder friendship. Sometimes it is assumed that a man should leave his friends behind when he marries. His wife will be his best or even his only friend. Such an attitude is tragic for friendship but even more so for marriage. If there is a way to doom a marriage with overloaded expectations, it is to say that husband and wife will be all that the other needs in friendship, support, and understanding. Both husband and wife need friends and support, partly to help them discover how to treat each other.

Frequent moves from one part of the country to another make it difficult to form deep friendships. Rushed schedules, long work days, and lengthy commuting times impede friendships. A very strong suspicion that friends are neither necessary nor possible gets in the way.

You may have heard the saying that friendship doubles life's joys and halves life's sorrows. Without close friends, we are the losers on both counts.

What Kinds of Friendships Do I Have? Are They OK?

No doubt, I am making this issue appear to be a more serious problem than most of us feel. All of us have friends. These friendships may vary in depth, duration, and what we can ask of each other, but for what they are, the friendships feel good. Let's catalogue the types of friendships that may be common among us males.

We all know people who *create a friendly atmosphere*. The manager of a filling station, the clerk of a convenience store, the folks at the dry cleaners—these people can greet you in such a way that your day is brighter, and you walk out full of smiles. Recently I spent a few days as a patient in a hospital, my first ever. Most of the time I was on complete bed rest, having to ask for every need. The folks who cleaned my room and made my bed, the ones who brought my food, the nurses, aides, and technicians—all filled my life with tenderness and hope at a painful and scary time. I will not likely see any of them again. And yet, at a time when I needed them, they were true friends.

Then there are friends who *do favors for each other*. These might be neighbors who loan each other tools or water each other's lawns and keep an eye on the house during vacations.

They might be co-workers who cover each other's phones or pick up the other's slack when a person is sick or has an emergency.

Some persons express deep feelings and meet their friends' needs by doing things. When my mother died and I needed to be away for an extended time, a friend called and said, "There's something I'd like to do for you. Your lawn will be mowed and your yard cared for until you get back." When I came home from the hospital after surgery, a friend became aware of the added workload for my wife, Mary Ann. He called around and arranged for various friends to bring us hot evening meals that would meet the requirements of my new dietary regimen. The first one arrived on my first night home—how nurturing it was to receive that gift! For many, both men and women, the language of friendship is, "If there is anything I can do, don't hesitate to call"—or they simply anticipate the need and meet it.

Again, there are friends with whom we *share activities*. With some it may be one special interest: hunting, fishing, basketball, football, tennis, nightclubbing, attending a concert or play. For a number of years, I met with a group to play basketball on Friday mornings, my day off. For the most part, they were younger and better players than I. And yet in our pickup games, there was a place for me. When things clicked with a particular team, we felt a high that only athletes know—even though it was only a pickup game in a tiny gym. We joshed, teased, insulted, criticized each other. Never did anyone take offense. It was part of the fun! We were our own referees. Hotly contested calls were settled by having one contender take a shot from the top of the key. I knew these men in no other setting and have not seen them since that gym closed for us. I really enjoyed that group, and years later, I still miss them.

Further, there are *friends from the past*. These are folks we treasure from a particular time in life—perhaps from our time in high school, military service, college. At one time we shared our ups and downs with them, and we love to see them occasionally, to recall those times. Sometimes we can reconnect and reengage in the present. Sometimes we cannot. Either way, these people enriched our lives then and have a special niche in our memories.

In addition to these, Jack Balswick discusses four male friendship structures that some find possible—notwithstanding the barriers we've mentioned, particularly competition and homophobia. One structure is that embracing the *good ol' boys*. These friendships may well have begun during childhood and are nurtured through the trials, pains, and triumphs of growing up. A good ol' boy will stick with his buddies through thick and thin. Such friends may sit around and talk a lot, but they rarely communicate personal feelings. They swap stories, humor, wisdom, and probably perpetuate male stereotypes. These friendships can be deeply meaningful and supportive, and yet such friends may be unable to express emotions even in a time of great crisis and tragedy.

A second structure is the *locker-room buddies*. These friendships go beyond those of friends who share activities. This group may have bonded as a team or a military unit. They may have cooperated in reaching a difficult goal. They may have tasted the bitterness of defeat and the ecstasy of victory together. From this common experience, they achieve a level of emotional sharing with each other that goes beyond what the good ol' boys typically achieve. They are more comfortable with each other than with women. After a hard day of work together, they may relax and say things among these friends they would not say anywhere else. They may hug each other after a touchdown or weep and express affection after a victory. Bantering, teasing, and humorous name-calling make up another part of the locker-room camaraderie. This sort of talk probably disguises closeness and affection. Once in a while, locker-room buddies may express emotions openly to each other, but for the most part, expression of emotion is coded and guarded.

Still another male friendship structure involves *sidekicks and "topkicks."* Tonto and the Lone Ranger, Robin and Batman, Watson and Sherlock Holmes are examples. In these relationships, the competition problem is solved: one man is clearly superior, the leader. Each is loyal to the other and would risk his life for the other's sake. In my youth and my young adult years, I have been both topkick and sidekick. At times I had a loyal friend who wanted to hang around with me, listen to my thoughts, join in whatever I was up to. At other times, I was very loyal to someone I saw as being more outgoing and assured with women, more confident—or who had a car when I did not. It is true that relating to another person in this way solves lots of competition issues.

The fourth pattern Balswick notices is that of *mentor-novices*. Often involving two persons of different ages, it is a hierarchical relationship based on an inequality of knowledge or skill. The mentor, assumed to be wiser, has the higher place in the relationship and passes on knowledge and wisdom to the novice. On a more profound level, the mentor supports the novice's development and well-being.[7]

We usually think of the older person as being the mentor, but at times the mentor can be younger. For example, as I try to develop and use computer skills, a younger friend who is a professional in this field has been a very generous and gentle mentor to me. When I try to understand the changing generations—for example, when I try to plan effective programming for Baby Boomers or Generation X-ers—younger pastors and church members teach me.

But frequently the more traditional pattern is seen. A younger colleague and I enter into a relationship, where, from time to time, I am asked to share of my wisdom and experience. I'm not quite sure how a mentoring relationship begins. Sometimes a former student calls me. Sometimes a fellow professional asks me for brief or systematic suggestions or supervision. Though honored to be a mentor, I must not overreach and offer more than that for which I am asked. A mentor is to encourage the other, not to take over the other's problems or struggles. And I need to know that mentors may be "fired" when they are not needed anymore. If we have done our mentoring well, we are prepared to go on to some other kind of friendship. And mentoring does not occur only between males. Some of my mentors have been women, and I have been a mentor to some women.

More mentoring is needed in this world. Adolescent boys, young adult men, folks struggling to find a first job, people trying to make it in their profession—all of these could use mentors who are invested in promoting their welfare.

Is There More?

I value each kind of friendship I have mentioned. And yet, rich as they are, these are not enough. Indeed, what enriches me in such friendships makes me hunger for an even greater closeness, a soul-touching closeness. In the Bible stories with which I began, we saw a greatness, a depth of commitment in those friendships. I long for a similar friendship that fits my day and my need.

As I stretch to describe this need and possibility, I offer a few quotations and definitions. Dinah Maria Mulock Craik captures an important aspect of friendship in her description (parts of which I have also seen in an Arabian proverb):

> Oh, the comfort—the inexpressible comfort
> of feeling safe with a person.
> Having neither to weigh thoughts,
> Nor measure words—but pouring them
> All right out—just as they are—
> Chaff and grain together—Certain that a faithful hand will
> Take and sift them—Keep what is worth keeping—
> And with the breath of kindness
> Blow the rest away.[8]

A plaque titled "A Friend" contains these words: "A friend is one who knows you as you are, understands where you've been, accepts who you've become and still gently invites you to grow."[9]

Frank Pittman quotes his dad, who sadly discovered that though he had many friends to "do things with," he didn't have those with whom he could speak deeply. Said his dad, "Your friends aren't necessarily the people you do things with, your friends are the people who know you too well and like you anyway."[10]

One of my helpful definitions of friendship is a paraphrase of Tom Dunn, my onetime counseling supervisor. Tom would remind me, "Therapy is where you go to be held accountable for your bull___." With my deepest and most trusted friends, friendship is where I go to be held accountable. I—and other males along with me—am a lesser person if I don't go either to friends or to therapy to be held accountable!

And yet I must add a caution to this description. Therapy is not a substitute for friendship, or friendship for therapy. Though I may need a therapist at times, I need friends *always*. The therapist holds me accountable out of professional commitment; my friends do the same out of love. And friends do more. According to two definitions that I recently heard, a friend is "someone who, when you've made a fool of yourself, doesn't think you've done a permanent job," "someone who knows the song in your heart and sings it to you when you forget." In addition to accountability, my friends offer me forgiveness, freedom from shame, gentle encouragement, and love.

Sam Keen, author of *Fire in the Belly*, has described the essence of such friendships:

> Friendship, *philia,* brotherly love, the affection that exists only between equals, is at once the most modest and rugged of the modes of love. It is quiet as an afternoon conversation, but strong enough to survive the acids of time. And while it draws us into our emotional depths, it demands no romantic frenzy. No howling at the moon, no explosions of contradictory feelings. No jealousy. Friendship creates gentle men and women. It depends upon nothing so fragile as a pretty face or fancy figures in a bank account, or so irrational as the thick sinews of blood and kin. It is based upon the simplest of the heart's syllogisms: I like you, you like me; therefore we are friends. And while we can imagine a satisfying life without the juicy overflow of sexual love or the sweet burdens of family, we know intuitively that without a friend the best of lives would be too lonely to bear.[11]

Keen describes his friend Jim of many years and concludes,

. . . we no longer live in geographical proximity. But the intimacy between us has remained. No matter what happens, our friendship has given us a kind of living immortality. So long as either of us lives we will never be anonymous, unknown, or unsung. Our stories are intertwined in the DNA of our friendship.[12]

Not only the Bible stories but these moving quotations help me clarify what I look for in a person that may be a close friend, a best friend, partner in the deepest friendship. I want a person who accepts me and likes me. I know it will take time, but I want as a friend a person whom I accept unconditionally and who accepts me unconditionally. This needs to be a person around whom I need do no pretending.

Further, this needs to be a person I can trust—I mean really trust. I want to be able to talk about secrets and know both that they won't be repeated and that they won't be ridiculed. I want to be able to confess my failures, admit my shames, say out loud my fantasies.

I hope this will be a person who will tell me when I'm all wet or when I've done wrong or when I can do better. These are touchy subjects. And therefore it's great if the friend can tell me such things in such a manner that I know the friend is on my side whether I heed the counsel or not. And if I do not, I hope for a friendship that endures, despite my faults.

I hope for many of the things found in those friendships of which I spoke earlier—may there be kidding, humor, and laughter; good times; shared interests; and long, open-ended talks. But most of all I hope for a friendship in which we are committed to being there for each other when needed. Truly, it is friendship that makes this world a warm, hospitable place.

What Are the Ways to Find and Make Close Friends?

I can speak of what I want in a friend because I have had a few friends. Probably none of us will have more than a handful of such friends in a lifetime. If we have had even one, we can count ourselves fortunate. Folks have noted that most males form these close friendships in adolescence or in the young adult years and that they find it very difficult to form them after that. That is true for me—I met most of my closest friends in my teens or twenties, and those friendships have persisted through the years.

And yet the present also holds possibilities for friendships of more depth than most of us currently experience. Each of us will need to find his own way on this, but I offer here some thoughts that make sense to me.

We need to begin with the recognition of our need. "Do I have friends of the depth, openness, and commitment that I desire?" Live with that question. It's easy to deceive ourselves in the midst of easy camaraderie with a number of people. Or we may be able to name a friend or two with whom we have shared such intimacy. But these folks may live in a different place, and they may have been such friends in a different time. As John Landgraf points out, we are wise to have one such friend in our present setting, within our local phone district!

Continue with two additional recognitions: (1) this friendship will not be identical to those among women that I may have noticed, admired, and envied; (2) this friendship will probably need to be different from the vast majority of my other male friendships.

Women often have things in their friendships that those of many males will not. They see each other frequently and often discuss small encounters in considerable detail. They explore feelings and analyze relationships with a considerably wider repertoire of feelings than we men usually have. Their encounters may include much more eye-to-eye contact than men want. These are all wonderful qualities in a friendship, but the value of a friendship is not negated simply because it lacks some of those characteristics.

Men's friendships can conceivably involve less frequent contact, less exchange of information, infrequent expression of emotions, and little or no eye contact and still be genuinely supportive. We need to find our own way. Perhaps our times of greatest intimacy will be when we sit and talk between sets of tennis. Perhaps, for the most part, we kid, joke, and play until one of us gives a signal of needing something more from the other.

And yet the friendships we are talking about are different from most we have experienced. We need to have some sort of agreement: if you really need me, I will be there; if you need to talk about something that is troubling you, I will listen; if you need to explore uncomfortable stuff, I am willing to support you in that exploration. These things take some doing.

OK, I've recognized the need to have at least one friend or more in my local phone district. I've also recognized that the friendship I seek will not be identical to women's deep friendships, and it will be different from most of my male friendships. What next? There are three possible alternatives: *courting, evolving,* or *testing.*

John Landgraf has suggested that sometimes one needs to *court* a new friend. That is, be intentional; be aware of what I am looking for in a friend. Then identify the person who has these characteristics and ask directly if that person is open to a deeper friendship with you. John recalls a time when he did just that. He had moved a thousand miles from his old friends to a new job, and he was lonely. He made several false starts in locating persons who might be close friends. Then he found someone he really wanted as a friend. This was a wise, thoughtful man, in many ways a private person, but one who had many commitments and a marriage to tend. John strongly suspected that this man was too busy to take him on as a friend. Nevertheless, he mustered his courage and invited the man out to lunch. John recalls,

> As the small talk played out and lunch was served, we both fell into silence. It was my move. Looking more at my plate than at him . . . I said softly, "I've been watching you from afar for some time. I like what I see. I am seeking a friend, and the reason for this lunch is to ask you to consider becoming my friend. I don't know how close we'd want to get or what form our friendship would take, but we could

start now and see where it wants to go. If you can make
time for an occasional meeting like this and are willing to
try . . ." As my voice trailed off I looked up—to see him
crying! He was lonely too. No one had ever approached him
this way. He was touched. We became fast friends. What a
great feeling![13]

Intentionality, specific identifying and inviting—courting, if
you will—may be one doorway to these deep friendships.

Yet another way may be *evolving* from any of the other
kinds of friendship we have mentioned. Life is experienced
together, history is shared, support is given, and two men
draw closer together. One of the great friendships of my life
evolved. Lee and I met when we were seniors in high school.
We had come to a state Christian youth convention and been
assigned to stay together. With great loneliness and urgency
we compared our lives and talked into the night. Neither
of us thought the other was much fun! The next fall we met
again as freshmen at a small liberal arts college, leading
to four years of memorable experiences. We played on the
same terrible football team, sang in the same good choir,
went on trips and tours, sometimes competed for the same
women, and sometimes double-dated. We enjoyed many
laughs, jokes, and pranks together. I stood up with him at
his wedding.

The friendship appeared to have a terminal point as we
selected graduate schools. From the Midwest, he headed for
Berkeley, and I was bound for Boston. But we kept in touch
and, in time, lent support to each other in our profession.
Our friendship evolved. I will tell more of it a little later.

Sometimes deeper friendship comes through *testing* the
limits of the old friendship. Another of the great friendships
of my life, my relationship with Ron, happened in this way.
We had known each other for a number of years, had shared
a number of activities and experiences, and enjoyed each
other's company. And then came an evening I will always
remember. It was late at night. He was a guest in my home,
and everyone else had gone to bed. As we chatted, he started
talking about some deep, hurting places in his life. The

topics he discussed were items over which we had joked many times and on which he had stirred much laughter with his sarcasm and irony. But this time it was different. He had taken some measure of me, decided I could be a reliable friend, and trusted me. He talked for a long time. I don't think I did much more than listen. I am quite sure he felt some relief in the talking. What I know is that our friendship moved to a new level. Quite soon there came a time when we openly said that we could say anything we needed to each other. It started that evening.

Courtship, evolving, testing—these may be the doors to that deeper friendship. Then comes enjoying the journey and keeping the promises.

Can Men Be Friends with Women?

What about friendships with women? As one male put it, "If I eliminate women from my potential friendships, I lose half the human race, and some of the most fascinating possibilities at that." There are a few hazards, difficulties, and misunderstandings to face and many rewards to enjoy from including women in our close friendships.

One issue is that of sexual attraction and possible romance between the two. If both persons are single, a relationship may begin in delightful ambiguity—some of the things one looks for in a friend are also desirable in a romantic partner. In many friendships, either or both will be married. Though attraction and warm feelings may be a part of the enjoyment, there will need to be a much clearer agreement. The attraction is OK, but we will keep the expression of such attraction within boundaries that feel appropriate to both of us and to our spouses.

Yet another issue may be conducting the friendship in such a way that it doesn't have to contend with rumor or suspicion. Openness with spouses and comfort about the importance of such friendships are important first steps. Fitting times to spend time together are also important. For example, I have found few eyebrows raised about breakfasts, luncheons, or coffee. Many persons do that. Other settings that might look more like a date may create problems.

The rewards of such friendships are great indeed. Stimulating intellectual conversations, sharing of resources by persons in similar fields of employment, help in understanding the mysteries of the other gender, mutual celebration over joys and support in hard times—all of these and more await the men who make the effort to form nonromantic friendships with women. Sam Keen put it forcefully: "At the present moment in history, friendship between men and women is one of the great untapped resources for renewing the world."[14]

Can Men's Groups Be Part of the Answer to My Search for Friendship?

Men may find great enjoyment in a wide variety of men's groups. These groups may have about as wide a variety as that of male friendships. And, as male friendships differ from female friendships, male groups will differ from female groups.

Some men's groups may come together after sharing an activity or working on a project together. I've known folks that feel much closer to each other after spending a few Saturdays on a Habitat for Humanity project or hours preparing a drama. A group that enjoys fishing, hunting, golf, tennis, or rehearsing and performing music may develop a deeper closeness from time spent together.

While men's groups may be "face to face" in a circle at times, they may be "side to side" at other times. As a matter of fact, there are many things men like to do side by side—paint a house, take a walk, do dishes after a church supper, sing in a chorus or quartet, or play in a band or orchestra. I am reminded of the story of a man who was trying to get closer to his father. He went home and tried sitting and talking with him, but this was not working. Finally, he suggested to his father that they take a walk in the woods as they had done in the past. They went out, walked side by side for four hours without speaking, and came back with the sense of a wonderful bond between them. Men may discover themselves growing together doing group activities side by side.

For a time at least, men's groups may want to be larger, relaxed, and low-key. In the church where I serve, a popular new men's gathering is based on a model brought by one man from his former church. Once a month any men who want to (and the group usually includes males from ages nine to ninety) gather for a meal prepared by some of the men. They sit and chat at round tables. A simple program is followed each month. We sing a bit. One man brings a brief devotion including personal witness. Another is the "man of the month" and tells us some things about his life, work, family, interests, values. (Each of these has a ten-minute limit.) Next is a speaker of some interest—perhaps a well-known athlete, a TV commentator, a representative of a community service organization. Then there is a brief business session with occasional opportunities for men to volunteer to serve at various tasks. After a closing prayer, we are on our way. After a year, men in the church know each other better, bring friends and family members to this "less churchy" event, and enjoy being together. It has value in itself and may be the means by which some men will want to become even closer.

All of the good in these kinds of groups may not satisfy a deeper hunger. The longing for communion, the loneliness, the problems and confusions of being a man may lead us to seek a trusting and trustworthy men's group. Such a group may start when I feel this need and find one other man who is seeking something similar. Together we may identify some others that might like such a group. We meet together, form a group, and explore life together.

Philip Culbertson tells of entering into such a group. He had been thinking of and wanting such a group for quite some time. But when a friend, a student of his, came with deeper cries and greater hurts than one person could respond to, he felt the time was ripe. Together they thought of others who might want such a group and invited them together for an evening to explore the possibility. One had been in a group before, and one had read a good bit about such groups. Others came without any such knowledge or experience. They talked about the things they would need to agree on. At the first meeting they could identify some agreements, but others were made as the group went on. They agreed on a policy of absolute confidentiality: nothing said in the group, even the most innocent statements, would be repeated outside. Another thing they would need of each other was trust, and another was agreeing not to miss a meeting unless it was absolutely unavoidable.

They also met at the same time and place each week, and agreed to a two-hour limit. They agreed to live with the process and not to set goals for the group. They would, as far as they could, tell the truth. No one would be forced to tell anything he did not wish, but when a person spoke on the topic under discussion, it was expected that he would be honest with himself and others. They agreed not to use their valuable time to discuss the things men often talk about— for instance, sports. They also agreed to try to talk in "I-statements"—about feelings, disappointments, hopes, inadequacies, joys, failures, and fears. ("I-statements" are phrased in terms of what *I* feel and experience not in terms of observations of others.) Further, they agreed that each person shared responsibility for keeping the focus on their original purpose—to be honest, open, and supportive of each other.

The men met together for two years, before graduations and transfers meant that the group as it existed would need to end. As they look back, they wish for even more transparency—Culbertson wishes particularly that they could have talked more about prayer and the spiritual life. Far exceeding any regrets, however, was the joy in the strength, the community, the peace that this group of men found in each other.

Culbertson says that invariably when he tells the story of this group, men say, "Oh, how I wish I could have a group

like that!" His response is this: "You can if you will but take
the risk. The quest is worth every frightening bit of effort."[15]

A Celebration and a Tear

As I have been exploring the topic of friendship with you, my
heart's eye keeps going back to a particular friend—Lee.
Earlier I told you of meeting him in high school, of being
college classmates and buddies, and of keeping contact alive
through graduate school and our early careers. When we got
together at conferences or retreats as young pastors, we
discovered that the old enjoyment of each other was there.
Indeed it was all the more precious as we were often lonely
and unsure trying to get a start in our professions. I would
write him from time to time. He would more often pick up the
phone and call. Sometimes our work would bring us together—such as giving leadership at a youth camp. Sometimes one would invite the other to his church for some event.
We always did what we promised, but we felt that the
greatest gain was in the time spent together. The years and
decades passed, and we became even more aware how rare
trusting, persisting friendships are and how much we valued
ours.

Lee was intense. He was much more outgoing than I. He
wanted excitement; if nothing was going on, he tended to
make things happen. I enjoyed many things about him, but
above all his creative and zany sense of humor. His sense of
the ridiculous was wonderful! Many a time I would call him
to complain with great intensity about some problem or
injustice. More often than not, he would hear the silliness in
the situation, burst out laughing, and in time get me gig-
gling about it as well. I often needed the perspective that his
gift of humor gave.

One time Lee called me with a piece of personal news. He
was pleased but a bit embarrassed that the seminary from
which he had graduated and where he supervised field education wanted to confer an honorary doctorate on him. He
was embarrassed because all our lives, honorary degrees
were among the things we poked fun at! I assured him that

this honor was well deserved, and if possible I would attend the event. I did just that, along with two other lifelong friends, Ron and Marjorie Erickson. What a celebration we had! Lee and Barb met us at the airport in a limousine! We laughed and sang into the night each of the evenings we were there. We stood proudly with our friend as he was honored for significant service in ministry and the training of ministers.

I was a bit shocked, though, at how ashen his complexion was. We had some frank discussions in which he admitted that some health problems were worsening. He also said that we had not been keeping in touch closely enough and that we should talk each week. So we did that—practically every week for the next twelve weeks. And then came a phone call from Barb to say that Lee had died that morning. He was fifty-six. We had been friends for nearly forty years.

That was seven years ago. I still miss him. Only in the last couple of years have I ceased the habit of picking up the phone and starting to dial him with some "mad, sad, or glad" piece of news as I used to do—and then remembering that I can't do that anymore. More and more, the events and chuckles that we shared surface in my memory, and I am filled again with wonder and joy that I had such a friend. The pain and sorrow of losing him are not too great a price to pay for that gift of friendship. Such friendship as that is a constant reminder that I am ever enfolded in the constant love of God.

Invitations

As you reflect on the gift of friendship, you may want to

__ affirm to a friend how much the friendship means to you

__ take steps to help a friendship grow deeper, through courtship, evolving, or testing

__ offer yourself as an interested older friend or mentor to a child, a youth, or a young adult

__ form a men's group of some sort

__ investigate joining a men's group of some sort

__ Write your own promises:

_____

_____

Questions for Conversation and Group Discussion

1. Make a list of your best friends. Give yourself time to make the list as complete as you can. For each friend, note four things: (a) when your friendship began; (b) what you admire most about this friend; (c) what you most enjoy doing with this friend; and (d) what you see as the growth opportunities for this friendship. Discuss any discoveries from this exercise with others in the group.

2. Do you belong to any men's groups? How would you describe them?

3. How did you feel about the men's group that Philip Culbertson described near the close of this chapter?

Resources

Balswick, Jack. *Men at the Crossroads: Beyond Traditional Roles and Modern Options.* Downers Grove, Ill.: InterVarsity Press, 1992.

Barclay, William. *The Letters to Timothy, Titus, Philemon.* Edinburgh, Scotland: Saint Andrew Press, 1956.

Culbertson, Philip. *Counseling Men.* Minneapolis: Fortress Press, 1994.

————. *New Adam: The Future of Male Spirituality.* Minneapolis: Fortress Press, 1992.

Keen, Sam. *Fire in the Belly: On Being a Man.* New York: Bantam Books, 1991.

Kipnis, Aaron R. *Knights without Armor: A Practical Guide for Men in Quest of Masculine Soul.* New York: Jeremy P. Tarcher/Putnam Book, G. P. Putnam's Sons, 1991.

Landgraf, John R. *Singling: A New Way to Live the Single Life.* Louisville: Westminster/John Knox, 1990.

Oliver, Gary J. *Real Men Have Feelings Too.* Chicago: Moody Press, 1993.

Olson, Richard P. *Changing Male Roles in Today's World: A Christian Perspective for Men—and Women Who Care about Them.* Valley Forge, Pa.: Judson Press, 1982.

Pittman, Frank III. *Man Enough.* New York: G. P. Putnam's Sons, 1993.

Smith, David W. *The Friendless American Male.* Ventura, Calif.: Regal Books, GL Publications, 1983.

Sparks, James Allen. *Friendship after Forty.* Nashville: Abingdon Press, 1980.

Weber, Stu. *The Tender Warrior: God's Intention for a Man.* Sisters, Oreg.: Multnomah Books, Questar, 1993.

Notes

1. Philip Culbertson, *New Adam: The Future of Male Spirituality* (Minneapolis: Fortress Press, 1992), 89.

2. Ibid., 89-90.

3. Some Bible scholars will question my weaving together various parts of the New Testament in this story. Second Timothy appears to be written quite late—in honor of Paul, not by Paul. I admit that my story is speculative. Still it seems to me that the verses I cite have an authentic feel of real need. The reader will have to decide.

4. William Barclay, *The Letters to Timothy, Titus, Philemon* (Edinburgh, Scotland: Saint Andrew Press, 1956), 250.

5. Leonard Sweet, *The Jesus Prescription for a Healthy Life* (Nashville: Abingdon Press, 1996), 39-40.

6. Ibid., 39.

7. Jack Balswick, *Men at the Crossroads: Beyond Traditional Roles and Modern Options* (Downers Grove, Ill.: InterVarsity Press, 1992), 177-84.

8. R. F. Smith, "A Friendship and Safety," *The Columns*, 25 July 1993 (Huntington, W. Va.: Fifth Avenue Baptist Church).

9. David W. Smith, *The Friendless American Male* (Ventura, Calif.: Regal Books, GL Publications, 1983), 182.

10. Frank Pittman III, *Man Enough* (New York: G. P. Putnam's Sons, 1993), 179.

11. Sam Keen, *Fire in the Belly: On Being a Man* (New York: Bantam Books, 1991), 173-74.

12. Ibid., 173.

13. John R. Landgraf, *Singling: A New Way to Live the Single Life* (Louisville: Westminster/John Knox, 1990), 117.

14. Keen, *Fire in the Belly*, 216-17.

15. Philip Culbertson, *Counseling Men* (Minneapolis: Fortress Press, 1994), 144-52.

5

Husbands

Something more and different is expected of him than used to be. At the same time, much more wisdom and insight are available to him in recent years. It is also true, however, that the stresses, strains, and demands on him have grown considerably. Many—nearly half—who attempt to do what he does fail, and yet he keeps trying. If he fails, he may well try again. He is an endangered species, but he is willing to risk. For he knows there is so much to be gained if he succeeds.

Whom do I describe? A *husband* in twentieth- and twenty-first-century America. Tim Allen's relationship with his wife on the *Home Improvement* TV show is an example of the marriage struggle for many of us. In episode after episode, he misses something important and offends, hurts, or irritates his wife, Jill. But then he gains a new perspective from Wilson, his guru. With imperfect understanding but boundless good-will, he somehow reconciles and renews his relationship with Jill by the time the show ends. Would that such marital misunderstandings ended the same way for all of us!

Frankly, I approach this subject with humility and wish I could tell you more about performing this role well. I should be informed about husbands—I have been one for nearly two-thirds of my life. By the time this is printed, Mary Ann and I will have observed our fortieth wedding anniversary and have noted the fifteenth, tenth, and sixth anniversaries of our children's marriages. I have conducted nearly four hundred weddings and spent time with most of those couples before their weddings and with many of them after. I have done considerable marriage counseling and conducted marriage renewal retreats. Marriage is a topic that fascinates me.

For all of this, I well know that being a good husband is more art than science, more mystery than certainty. I have known couples whose marriages—from my perspective—should have succeeded but failed and others whose marriages I thought were going to fail but which succeeded. Further, who knows what goes on in the soul of another couple's marriage? How is success or failure measured? Certainly God's grace and blessing are a part of every successful marriage.

At the same time, we can be helped by some basic wisdom. We know some general things about being husbands. Also, a man can learn ways to be a good fit, a matched set with the woman with whom he shares life. As you know, I cannot give you a surefire "how-to" manual guaranteed to make your marriage great. I can, however, give you important information and guidelines that will not hurt and may help. Quite possibly, this information will help you build—or rebuild or renew—a rich marriage with your spouse.

Not all of us are husbands. At any given moment only half of us men over age eighteen are married. Many of the rest of us were married and are no longer, or will be at some future time. The role of husband is one that most of us experience for some time in our lives. Failing at it brings great pain, both to others and to ourselves. Succeeding at it answers some of the deepest longings of our hearts. There is so much we hope for, so much to gain. We don't want to fall into dull routine or uneasy truce in our marriages as so many do.

How can I be husband to my wife in a way that opens the door to the beautiful possibilities—the rich love, friendship, romance—of marriage? That is a question worth asking! It is an assignment deserving great thought and hard work.

And so, let's explore. First we will talk about what the Bible says. Then, out of those learnings, we'll think further about the basics of a good marriage. And finally we will consider some of the new and hard issues we face with our wives in today's changing world.

What Does the Bible Say?

Let's take a look at two Bible chapters that provide a basis for our discussion of marriage. The first is Genesis 2.

In the stories of creation, we are told, "Then the LORD God said, 'It is not good that the man should be alone; I will make him a helper as his partner'" (v. 18). The woman is to be the man's helper. Far from implying a subordinate role, the term *helper* suggests an empowering task. This word *helper* is often used of almighty God who is present and helps frail humanity. God promises to create a godlike empowering presence for the man and does so by causing the man to sleep, taking a rib from him, and forming the woman. When God brings the woman to the man, the delighted man exclaims, "This at last is bone of my bones and flesh of my flesh" (v. 23). These words might be paraphrased, "Wow! I find myself in you!" And the passage concludes, "Therefore a man leaves his father and his mother and clings to his wife, and they become one flesh. And the man and his wife were both naked, and were not ashamed" (vv. 24-25).

These words are foundational teachings; they are quoted more often, both in the Bible and by others, than any others about the nature of marriage. God created woman and man for each other. God wills the bond between man and woman that we call marriage.

It is God's intent that two individuals create something new. This closeness, a oneness, is mysteriously called "one flesh" in marriage. The phrase suggests many things. In a "one flesh" marriage, the partners exhibit deep mutual respect and helpfulness. They share conversation and communication.

Two people know each other deeply and share life's goals. The phrase *one flesh* also implies an innocent, joyous sex life. It may convey a picture of a couple joined in intercourse, their bodies intertwined. In the divine intent, this sexual consummation is a fitting expression of all they commit to each other and all they share with one another. God intends this bond between man and woman to be even stronger than one's bond to parents. It is to be enriching and enduring. Such is marriage as God created it and wills it to this day.

The second Bible teaching is from Ephesians 5, a passage that has often been tragically misinterpreted. A misunderstanding occurs when people assume that this teaching begins in verse 22, "Wives, be subject to your husbands as you are to the Lord." Actually, the passage starts in verse 21: "Be subject to one another out of reverence for Christ." That is the major premise—mutual subjection. Out of that major premise follow two consequences, the way wives are to treat husbands and the way husbands are to treat wives.

"*Wives,* be subject to your husbands as you are to the Lord" (v. 22). In the original Greek, this sentence has no verb. It is clearly a dependent clause linked to the main clause in verse 21. The passage tells us that as the church is to relate to Christ, so wives are to relate to their husbands (vv. 22-24).

"*Husbands,* love your wives, just as Christ loved the church and gave himself up for her . . ." (v. 25; see vv. 25-33). Christ loved the church by sacrificing for it, dying for it, sustaining it. So husbands are to relate to their wives in a sacrificial, self-giving, nurturing way.

What Christ did for the church, the church is called to do for Christ. When we start at the right place in this passage and hear it clearly, no hierarchy is implied. Clearly, wives are not mandated to follow our leadership if it is ungodly or does not reflect Christ's love and sacrifice. The Ephesians text calls couples to mutual submission, mutual service, mutual sacrifice, mutual love, mutual care.

These two Bible passages point to a number of basic truths. For example, God entrusts tremendous power to the human relationship, especially the relationship called marriage. God created marriage for the welfare and happiness of humankind. God designed it to be mutually strengthening and mutually enriching. And God wills that it be enduring. We men who enter into marriage have a high and holy calling—the calling to be husband.

What Makes Good Marriages Today?

With those biblical teachings before us, our next step is to discover how to live out these great truths in our present setting. Let's start with the basics—What makes good marriages today? To answer that, I highlight a few insights from three helpful sources.

Warren Lane Molton gives us a place to begin when he suggests that married couples should be "friends, partners, and lovers."[1] These are not casual terms; they express the dimensions of a good and rich marriage. Each needs to be present, in balance with the others.

Married couples need to be *friends*. "Today I marry my best friend" is a statement often heard on wedding days. That wedding-day friendship needs to continue and grow throughout the couple's lifetime. In a healthy friendship, each knows the other, and both are known in ever greater depth. Mutual discovery and self-revealing go on. Trust needs to be present at the beginning, and that trust—including the willingness to share dreams, hopes, angers, fears, secrets, regrets—needs to develop further. Each needs to accept the other and the other's style and way of doing things. As time goes on, this task becomes more difficult; the other's habits and mannerisms can become annoying. Friends learn to accept such things (or maybe to communicate tactfully about them) and go on. Even more, married partners should *like* one another and enjoy one another's company. True friendship embraces all of these aspects.

Married couples are also *partners*—partners in the finances, the work, the child rearing of marriage. A couple needs to make and live out decisions about the use and management of money, about housing, about transportation, about recreation, about faith and worship.

Couples begin their marriage by making a sacred *covenant* with each other before friends and family and before God. The wedding vows are but part of that covenant that says, "we want to 'do life' together." This covenant is a mutual promise of equality, of commitment, of seeking shared goals for life.

Whether they know it or not, couples also make a *contract* with each other. A contract is the working agreement about how they expect to work out their covenant in everyday life. A couple has probably talked out parts of their contract. In other parts, each partner assumes that certain things will be carried out as they were in his or her own family. And some issues in a marriage need to be contracted or recontracted as they arise.

Molton has noted that sometimes a contract—this working agreement between a couple—may fall into difficulty. For example, one partner may want children, the other may not; or if they fail to have birth children, one may want to adopt, the other not. At times when the contract is in trouble, the couple is wise to return to their basic covenant (we promised each other to "do life" together) and strengthen it. Strengthening the covenant may draw them back to a renegotiated contract, a partnership with which they can live.

These two elements, friendship and partnership, are in balance in a good marriage. A partner's friendship can diminish if he or she feels that the spouse is not holding up the other end of the partnership. If one feels overworked, underappreciated, or unjustly treated, the friendship is apt to suffer. On the other hand, a couple can be so centered on a just partnership that they neglect the fun and delight of the friendship that originally drew them together. Friends and partners.

And *lovers*. Early in relationships most couples don't worry about this one. There is something electric between them; there is good chemistry; they are naturally drawn closer and closer together. Quite likely it is this chemistry that brought them together. At first it seems unimaginable that this bond will ever change or diminish. But change it does. A couple discovers that they must give attention to being lovers, or this vital dimension will diminish.

Couples can take steps to stay alive as lovers. Caring and praise and compliments are a good place to start. Celebration at each other's triumphs is important. Remembering and honoring special anniversaries is a good idea. (Many of us men have notoriously bad memories about special days that are important to the women we love and to us. Noting those days in advance in our planning calendars or using any other stimulus to the memory is a good idea.) Wise couples intentionally invest in special times away from children and other responsibilities. This is important for all couples but may be especially so for second marriages where the marriage has a shorter history than the parent-child relationships.

As we husbands move through the years in a marriage, we need to learn to use our *heads* as we seek to be romantic partners. Early in our relationship, I discovered that Mary Ann loved to receive a single rose. While we were dating and in the early years of our marriage, I sometimes simply found myself in a florist shop, buying her a rose. Now, years later, I need to use my head. When I am at my best, the thought occurs to me, "This has been a tense week for her. Maybe it's time for a rose." My spontaneous emotions don't propel me, but a head full of love can still guide me to the flower counter!

We males may think that we have established this loving relationship and can assume its continuation. Quite likely the women in our lives would like to hear us talk about it and reaffirm it. Something I often hear when I counsel couples is a wife's longing for her husband to be the lover he once was. The wife longs for simple gestures—a card, a note, a phone call, a small unexpected gift, a night out—anything that reassures her that she is special and that she is loved. Each of us men can consider this question: What in my words, my actions, my attitudes can convey to her, "You're still my romantic partner and I delight in you"?

Couples also need to work out what each wants and needs in romance. Many males feel that all romance should lead to intercourse, and the sooner the better. For many females, romance can have many expressions without intercourse. Closeness, touch, holding each other, tender words, lovely atmosphere (candlelight, for example), little gifts (a flower, a tape or compact disk, a bottle of bubble bath)—all lead to a satisfying intimacy.

Couples may misunderstand each other at times. Husbands may want more sexual expression and release within the marriage. Of course it may be the wife who feels this way, or the pattern can change in the course of a marriage.

There will be times when intercourse is not possible. Advanced pregnancy, the weeks following childbirth or surgery, necessary absences—these circumstances and others interrupt a couple's sex life. At other times intercourse may be difficult or impossible because of male problems. Certain medical conditions or medications can impair the male's ability to achieve an erection. If this happens, a man is wise to take two steps: (1) Admit and face the problem and seek medical counsel, difficult as this is to do. Much can be done to give relief to this medical problem. (2) Whether he gets relief or not, he should continue to romance his wife. A couple can have delightful romantic, sexual moments together without exchanging body fluids!

All of these "romance issues" deserve discussion and exploration by a couple. Romance has to do with enjoying and pleasing one's mate. Self-care so as to be attractive to the partner is important—baths, deodorants, appealing nightwear (or none if that pleases the partner). Attention can be given to planning a romantic setting (perhaps a romantic getaway) and a romantic atmosphere using lighting, music, flowers, incense or other exciting scents. Sensitive touch, perhaps a soothing massage—all this and more are part of being lovers.

One man who had been married a number of years told me, "In a long-term marriage, there is the wonderful gift of memory. We remember what has been shared and what has been survived! This memory enters into my wife's and my lovemaking. We often recall early sexual experiences as we partake in current ones."

Molton reminds us that couples who give attention and effort to being lovers may discover something even better than that first excitement. They may experience a love that is also secure and comfortable. Their romance is enhanced by a fulfilling marriage of growing as friends, as partners, and as lovers.

Another student of marriage, John Gottman, after careful research reaches a similar conclusion. He points out that what every person wants in a marriage is love and respect. As friends and lovers, they want love; as partners, they want respect. And they want those qualities communicated to them in a way that connects. (The tale about the husband who told his wife, "I told you I loved you on our wedding day. If I ever change my mind, I will let you know" points to what people *don't* want in marriage! If any of us has fallen into that, immediate steps should be taken. I would recommend starting with a card at an unexpected time and then going on from there.)

Gottman points out further that some "negativity"—some conflict, disagreement, or disappointment—in marriage is a good thing. (That's good to hear, because all of us will experience painful things in marriage at times.) However, positive factors and negative factors need to be held in healthy balance. With only positive factors, a marriage may become bland and routine. With too much negativity, a marriage may feel dangerous and hurtful. A proper ecology of marriage, he contends, involves a five-to-one ratio of positive to negative: there should be five times as much positive feeling and interaction as there is negative.[2] That may seem high, more of an ideal than a possibility. Still, Gottman contends, that is the atmosphere in which tensions can be constructively handled.

Love, respect, and creative tension (with the balance tipped on the side of positive factors)—these are the key elements in the strong marriages Gottman studied. I will mention one other study that provides light on our topic. Jeanette and Robert Lauer did a study for *Psychology Today* magazine titled "Marriages Made to Last." In this connection, they located more than three hundred couples who had been married fifteen years or more and who said their marriages were happy, successful, and enduring. These couples were interviewed and asked to select items from a questionnaire that best showed why their marriage had lasted. Here are some of the top-rated items:

My spouse is my best friend . . . I like my spouse as a person . . . Marriage is a long-term commitment . . . Marriage is sacred . . . We agree on aims and goals . . . My spouse has grown more interesting . . . I want the relationship to succeed . . . An enduring marriage is important to social stability . . . We laugh together.[3]

The Lauers found two common themes among these happily married couples: (1) They truly liked each other and showed this through such qualities as caring, giving, integrity, and a sense of humor; and (2) they shared a belief in marriage as both a long-term commitment and a sacred institution. These couples found marriage to be a task that sometimes demands gritting one's teeth and plunging ahead in spite of difficulties. One woman told them, "I'll tell you why we stayed together. I am just too darn stubborn to quit."

These folks remind us of the commonsense ingredients we need to put into our marriages: intentionality, constant effort, attention to the many dimensions of our spouse, and attention to our marriage tasks. The bad news from these studies is that marriage is hard work. The good news is that it can succeed! Marriage is alive and well for many persons. And help and wisdom are available to strengthen those marriage relationships.

Specifically, How Am I to Be an Effective Husband Today?

So far we have spoken of the sacredness of marriage and of good marriages in general. But married men today face a number of issues and opportunities that did not exist in the past. Let's talk about some of these.

1. How do two-career marriages change the role of husband?

It is now estimated that in 70 percent of all marriages, both husband and wife are employed outside the home. This percentage has doubled in the last forty years. It includes couples across the life span. Women are quite likely to be employed throughout their lifetimes, including during pregnancy, during the infancy and early years of their children, and until retirement. Women are also entering an ever wider range of careers, including many that require an investment of education, time, and energy equal to or greater than that required by their husbands' careers.

How do these facts affect husbands? A wife's employment may ease a tight financial picture for a family (although probably less than they expect), or it may provide money for more options. Her employment and financial power may also bring a change in the balance of authority and decision making in some households. And these changes may fuel competition between husband and wife.

The biggest change is the loss of her time for family and household matters and how this plays out in the marriage. Much has been written about women's "second shift." Writers describe studies showing that an employed woman continues to do about as much housework, cooking, and child care as she did before she was employed. At the same time, these studies reveal that husband and children have added very little to their list of responsibilities.

Yet some suggest that these studies do not look at enough factors. For example, a 1991 *Journal of Economic Literature* study reported that while wives do about seventeen more hours of work than their husbands do *inside* the home, the husbands do about twenty-two more hours of work (including commuting time) than the wives *outside* the home. Since, on the average, the present work week is longer for the man than the woman, the weekly employment-home investment for a woman is fifty-six hours; for a man sixty-one hours.[4] These studies may be useful in opening up a topic, but they are not much help in resolving a conflict in your marriage or mine. Several steps are useful for couples to take:

a. The husband needs to stop thinking about care of the house and children as his wife's responsibility. When he pitches in, he should not think of himself as helping her out. Rather he is taking his share of the couple's responsibility.

This issue affects the role of *partner,* but it has an impact on the *lover*'s role in marriage as well. John Gottman speaks of sex and housework as two marital hot spots, and he sees them closely intertwined.

Housework may seem like a trivial concern compared to sexuality, but women see it as a major issue affecting their sex life, as well as the overall equality of their marriage. I've interviewed newlywed men who told me with pride, "I'm not going to wash the dishes, no way. That's a woman's job." Two years later, the same guys asked me, "Why don't my wife and I have sex anymore?" They just don't understand how demeaning their attitude about housework is toward their wives. Treating your wife as a servant will almost inevitably affect the more intimate, fragile parts of a relationship. Being the sole person in a marriage to clean the toilet is definitely not an aphrodisiac![5]

b. The couple needs to talk about how each is feeling about the division of labor and what it would take to make it feel fair for each. The couple breaking out of old stereotypes concerning who does what work will need to look for new guidelines. They may find help in discussing these questions:

Who has the longest work week?
What tasks does one or both of us enjoy? What tasks does one or both of us dislike? At which tasks is one of us more skilled?

What does each partner need as "me" time or "fun" time? Is that acceptable to the other? How do we negotiate different standards of cleanliness or thoroughness in doing these tasks? (We men—and I include myself here—generally do cleaning more quickly, less thoroughly than our wives—my wife—would prefer.)

c. The couple needs to agree to a plan and to a period of time they will try the plan before renegotiating it. They need both set times and spontaneous times to talk about how this is going. The talk can keep them current with each other and prevent buildups of resentment.

d. The couple should build in flexibility and ways to make changes. Little is gained if we substitute a new set of rigid work-role expectations for an old set. Any number of reasons could exist to change a very good plan—one person's extra heavy or light schedule, the birth of a child or a child's departure for college, sickness or surgery, retirement, and so on.

e. A two-paycheck couple may want to stop and ask, "Why are we doing this?" If the answer is because the careers are fulfilling to both, they will want to continue. If the desire for more income is the primary reason, they may want to reconsider: How much net money is this arrangement bringing us? Is there something we can do without so that we reduce our expenses? Men who have escaped the rigid role expectations (mentioned in chapter 2) are free to consider being a househusband and primary care provider for a couple's children. A small but growing number of men have found this to be an attractive option—one way to overcome the father-child distance, of which I will speak in the next chapter.

Again, this doesn't have to be a once-and-for-all decision. At some periods of life having one partner stay home and provide a larger portion of home and child care may make a lot of sense. The stay-at-home person can be either wife or husband. We all have much to learn about husbanding in a two-career marriage. New ways to be friends, partners, and lovers need to be discovered.

2. I hear about "his marriage" and "her marriage." Do we want and need different things from marriage? What about differences in the ways women and men communicate?

I wondered what one of my daughters was telling me when I opened my birthday gift from her—Deborah Tannen's book titled *You Just Don't Understand!*[6] She explained (and I believe her) that she thought I would be interested in this best-selling book on women and men in conversation. A subsequent gift was another book with the startling title *Men Are from Mars; Women Are from Venus,* subtitled *A Practical Guide for Improving Communication and Getting What You Want in Your Relationships.*[7] These and other authors reveal striking discoveries about the mysteries of male-female communication. Years ago, I remember reading that husbands and wives miscommunicate with each other at least 20 percent of the time. On the basis of new research, these authors tell us that men and women miscommunicate much more than that *unless* they learn how differently men and women communicate and make efforts to talk across that barrier.

These miscommunications can have tragic results. Not understanding and not responding appropriately can frustrate people who genuinely love each other. This failure may cause their love to turn to indifference or hatred.

Here are some examples of difficulties in male-female communication:

a. Al and Maria have been out for a nice evening. Maria asks, "Would you like to stop for a bit of refreshment before we go home?" "No," Al responds. He is amazed when Maria is angry as they arrive home.

b. As Abe arrives home from work, Maggie asks him what happened at work, "Nothing much," he replies. Maggie learns that several people were dismissed that day. After Abe spends an evening with a mutual friend, and Maggie asks what is new in the friend's life, Abe answers, "Nothing." Later he mentions that the friend has become engaged. Maggie is hurt by Abe's failure to share information.

c. At a public meeting on the school system, John makes several statements and asks a number of questions while Martha sits silent. When they arrive home, Martha is eager to talk about the ideas presented at the meeting, but John is silent and withdrawn.

d. When Eve had a lump removed from her breast, she found it upsetting to have her body be cut into. She was also sad that the surgery had changed the contour of her breast. When she expressed this to women friends, they offered such responses as "I know. When I had my operation, I felt the same way" or " I know. It's like your body has been violated." When she told her feelings to her husband, Mark, he responded, "You can have plastic surgery to cover up the scar and restore the shape of your breast." Eve was comforted by her women friends but upset by Mark, even though he had been wonderfully supportive through the surgery.[8]

e. Jane says, "We never have any fun anymore." Jim responds, "That's not true—we both had several good laughs while watching TV last Friday." Jane continues, "We never go out." Jim explodes, "Why, just two weeks ago last Wednesday, I took you to dinner and a movie!" Each seems illogical and unreasonable to the other.

Such stories of misunderstandings, accumulated over the years, can cause a beautiful love-filled marriage to shrivel and die. How are we to understand what's going on and improve the situation?

Deborah Tannen points out that males and females grow up differently, are socialized differently, and so have quite different cultures regarding conversation. She uses some extremely broad generalizations to make this point. Tannen suggests that boys grew up loving to be outdoors and playing competitive games, probably in fairly large groups. Girls grew up relating to a single friend or a much smaller group. The friendship, not the competition, was the key concern. These differences continue into adulthood. Tannen summarizes:

If women speak and hear a language of connection and intimacy, while men speak and hear a language of status and independence, then communication between men and women can be like cross-cultural communication, prey to a clash of conversational styles. Instead of different dialects, it has been said they speak different genderlects.[9]

Deborah Tannen says that men and women speak *cross-culturally* and need to understand each other's manner of speaking, their *genderlects*. If both boys and girls are raised in a wide variety of ways, however, we have not two genderlects but many.

Further, John Gray contends that the male-female difference is even greater than Tannen suggests. With playful imagination, he suggests that our differences are interplanetary! He asks us to imagine that men are from Mars and women from Venus. When they first discovered each other,

The love between the Venusians and Martians was magical. They delighted in being together, doing things together, and sharing together. Though from different worlds, they reveled in their differences. They spent months learning about each other, exploring and appreciating their different needs, preferences, and behavior patterns. For years they lived together in love and harmony.[10]

Then, in Gray's fable, they came to earth and suffered amnesia. They forgot they were from different planets and were supposed to be different. Everything they had learned about their differences was erased from their memory. From that day on, men and women have been in conflict. (Does his parable sound familiar? Does it perhaps describe falling in love with a delightful woman and then trying to maintain a relationship with her for decades of marriage?)

What are the differences in the way men and women converse? Tannen and Gray mention a few basic ones. (Again, they are speaking in broad generalities of the ways men and women tend to converse and thus, at times, to miss each other.)

Women tend to engage in "rapport talk," that is, in talking out feelings and small interactions in some detail. The talk establishes rapport between those conversing. Men tend to engage in "report talk," that is, conversation that supplies basic information, gives advice, or solves a problem. For men, talk is often competitive.

Not understanding this, women may resent men's tendency to offer solutions, to try to fix things, as a too quick response to their pain. Men, though, may resent women's refusal to take actions to solve what they complain about, when the men may feel the solution is near at hand.[11] This is what is going on with Eve and Mark in example (d) above.

Men do more public speaking, and women do more private speaking. Public gatherings may provide a man opportunity to give advice, solve problems, establish status. Private speaking may be more comfortable for a woman, giving her a chance to share, reflect, connect. Or the woman may have experiences of not being heard or respected when speaking at public meetings. Each gender may be puzzled and hurt by these tendencies in the other, as with John and Martha in example (c) above. When the man is relatively quiet and mute at home, his wife may complain about his stinginess of spirit.

For the male, talk is information; for the female, talk is interaction. He may not talk until he has decided what he thinks about a subject. She may talk to find out what she thinks about a subject. He may need withdrawal, silence, privacy before he is ready to talk about things. She may need to talk about events right away in order to process them. Such misunderstandings were occurring between Abe and Maggie in example (b) above.

A woman's conversation may be more indirect and may include hints or clues that she hopes a partner will hear and respond to. She values intuition and hopes for it in her spouse. She will probably be disappointed. Men may need more direct requests to know what their wives would like of them. That is what was going on with Al and Maria in example (a) above.

Further, as John Gray points out, "To fully express their feelings, women assume poetic license and use various superlatives, metaphors, and generalizations. Men mistakenly take these expressions literally . . . and commonly react in an unsupportive manner."[12] This in turn leads to women's number-one complaint, "I don't feel heard." Unless we come to understand what she means by being heard, we are all too likely not even to understand the complaint! This is what was going on with Jane and Jim in example (e) above.

Many more differences exist, but these are some of the main ones. (Again, these descriptions will not fit every man, woman, or couple. If they do not fit you, consider yourself fortunate. If these do describe your spouse and you, you have much company.) And of course gender is only one source of different conversational styles. Various personality types and preferred use of either right or left brain also influence how people communicate.

One thing is certain: conversation and adequate communication are good for our marriages. What then can we do to improve them?

(1) Simply recognize the basic differences in the way men and women communicate and in what they probably want from conversation. Frequently ask your wife, "What do you mean?" and encourage her to ask you the same question. I can't overemphasize how important this question is for couples.

(2) Read over this information and the examples with your wife. Discuss which examples describe the two of you accurately and which do not.

(3) Make an attempt to listen more. Recognize that your wife very probably wants something different from your listening than you think. Ask her, "What would you like of me, to listen and support you or to give you suggestions and advice?"

(4) Make an attempt to talk more. Your wife may long for more information from you about where you are, what you are doing, what you are struggling with. She probably does not expect you to have a problem completely solved before you tell her about it.

(5) Be honest with her and with yourself when you cannot give either the listening or the talking she may want. John

Gray notes two things about us men: sometimes we need to go "into the cave," that is, to have some time alone. This may be for many reasons, but we are wise to withdraw when we need to. Further, men in relationships tend to be like rubber bands. After a time of intimacy, we tend to pull away and then later to snap back. These are normal male patterns. When we need to follow them, we are wise to give our wives a brief explanation, including that magic phrase, "It's not your fault." Also, "I'll be back" or "I'll be back (at a specified time) to listen or discuss."

These steps may improve our marriages considerably. Some years ago, attorney Louis Nizer wrote that he could look around in a restaurant and tell which couples were married and which were not. If the man was listening to what the woman was saying, they were not married! I shared this thought with a friend, and she suggested it might be even simpler than that—if they're talking at all, they're not married!

Equipped with this information, we certainly can do better. Tannen believes that we can gain from learning each other's conversation styles: "Many women could learn from men to accept some conflict and difference without seeing it as a threat to intimacy, and many men could learn from women to accept interdependence without seeing it as a threat to their freedom."[13] She concludes on a hopeful note:

> Understanding genderlects makes it possible to change—to try speaking differently—when you want to. But even if no one changes, understanding genderlect improves relationships. Once people realize that their partners have different conversational styles, they are inclined to accept differences without blaming themselves, their partners, or their relationships. The biggest mistake is believing there is one right way to listen, to talk, to have a conversation—or a relationship.[14]

3. Why are my wife and I hurting so much? Can we do a better job at handling conflict? Is there a way that we can reach an understanding about some of these painful differences?

A recent, well-researched article in *Health* magazine contends that the secret to a good marriage is not in religion, sex, or money. It is all in how the couple handles their conflicts. There is wisdom in that. Marriage engages two people on so many levels—friendship, finances, responsibilities, children, recreation, romance, sex. Certainly two people will have differences with each other, conflicts, and disappointments in each other. Will such differences become a means of growing together, or will they tear a couple apart?

Sometimes couples become so frustrated with each other that they hurt each other terribly. Spouse abuse—verbal, emotional, physical, and sexual—is an all too common fact in marriage today. This tragic behavior undoubtedly has a number of sources. If the partners saw such behavior or experienced such behavior from their parents, they are more likely to engage in it themselves. Isolation, the absence of persons to whom to turn, is a factor. Lack of a repertoire of ways to argue and settle differences makes abusive behavior all the more likely. Extreme stress—the loss of a job, too many unpaid bills, fatigue, more responsibilities than one can handle, a sick or crying child—can cause one to snap and be abusive. And yet we need to face the fact that men abuse their spouses and children much more than they do bosses or co-workers. Why? Because they can get away with it at home.

If you recognize yourself or some other family you care about in these paragraphs, I urge you to contact your pastor or a family-services professional. The health, life, and welfare of people are at stake.

Although many do not reach the point of engaging in abusive behavior, conflict is a given in all marriage relationships, and wise are those who learn to handle conflict well. A couple may begin by thinking about its conflict style. John Gottman points out that there are at least three styles of marriages, each of which can be healthy. Each style will have a corresponding conflict style.

Some couples are *validators*. When they have a conflict, say, over who should clean the kitchen, they will remain calm, consider all sides, air their views. They will try to understand why the other feels as he or she does and reach a compromise.

Some couples are *volatile.* These are romantic, dramatic, emotional folks. And they jump at the chance to have an explosive argument. Their arguments are frequent, lively, loud, passionate. Their making up after the "fight" is equally passionate.

And some couples are *conflict avoidant.* Such couples may disagree very seldom, perhaps once every few years, and may sidestep many issues. Even when they admit to differences, they don't necessarily need to find a middle ground. They may be content to agree to disagree.

Gottman has discovered that each type of couple can be happy as long as they maintain a healthy ratio (remember? five to one) of loving to conflictual exchanges. Couples who snap at each other frequently need a constant flow of loving moments for balance. Couples who bristle with conflict only once a year or so may need much less frequent professions of their love. And so here is a basic guideline for conflict: give and receive assurances of love and commitment to each other even as you face the conflict.

Of course couples may need to negotiate over their conflict style. One may be volatile; one may be an avoider. One may enjoy a good argument; one may dread it. We men are quite often the avoiders, withdrawing, fleeing, or falling silent when our wives bring up topics that call for conflict management. We will do well to admit the need for conflict and find a way to handle it. The first compromises may need to be over style—how often and freely do we conflict and in what manner?

Then we need to find a conflict procedure that fits the needs of both men and women. I once counseled an engaged couple that did very well together—until they had a conflict. Then everything went to pieces. I was not present to see what happened during these conflicts, and they were so upset that they could not accurately describe such times to me. Finally, I discovered a clue: the male had been a championship debater in college! When conflict arose, he went into that mode—scoring points, ignoring or rebutting points of the "opponent," demolishing the arguments of the opposition. Those are OK behaviors in a college debate tournament but not with a cherished, sensitive person with whom you hope to share a life! In seeking a conflict style, men often seek "rules of engagement" similar to those that govern a debate tournament, a court of law, a baseball game. If there are none, men don't know how to act. Most marriage conflict does not have rules of engagement—anything can happen anytime. That can be difficult—especially for a man. A couple needs to create its own commonsense way of managing conflict, a method that also honors a woman's need to express feelings, be listened to, and be heard.

Howard Markman, university professor and marriage re-treat leader, suggests that a couple develop and use a domes-tic version of *Robert's Rules of Order.* The pattern would be something like this. One person speaks at a time. First, the one with a problem or complaint speaks. The person should talk about any feelings connected to this issue but avoid personal attacks. Then the other person paraphrases what the spouse just said. This is to be sure that the problem has been heard and understood. There should be no defense or excuses. When the problem is thoroughly aired, then the two brainstorm for solutions. The couple selects what solutions they will try, and they schedule a time to see if the plan really worked.

The male temptation is not only to avoid facing the prob-lem but to skip over the problem quickly and race on to solutions. Markman urges men to resist this temptation. Benefits are gained from slowing down the discussion. Men often become the more upset in conflicts, and this slower pace may keep their hearts from pounding so hard. Also, being completely heard may be part of the solution for the woman and make any other solutions all the more attractive.

Markman suggests a simple structured process that in-cludes scheduled arguments; one person speaking at a time; careful listening; feedback, including paraphrasing and identification of feelings and issues; agreement on the problem; brainstorming for possible solutions; agreeing on one or more; and evaluating whether the problem is solved. Markman and partner Scott Stanley spend most of the first day of a two-day couples' workshop getting these simple techniques across. Near the end of the first day, they give each couple an assignment which, though it may seem strange, is based on solid marriage behavioral research. The assignment is not to use these techniques to solve a problem but rather to "agree on a plan to have fun and come back and tell us about it." The next morning, the couples pass descriptive notes to Stanley, and he reads what they did. They went shopping, made lists about what they liked about each other, went out to a special restaurant, had sex. There is a transformation in the group, and then they effectively practice the techniques of conflict management.

The conductors of these workshops have gathered proof that such training can increase the durability and quality of marriages. Anthony Schmitz, a contributing editor of *Health* magazine, notes,

> this, basically, is what behavioral marriage research has to offer in terms of hardheaded advice: Have fun together. Schedule your fights. Fight in a structured way to keep a lid on negatives and to keep the man of the house from turning into stone.[15]

Their careful research supports common sense. It also confirms some guidance given long ago in the book of Ephesians: "Be angry but do not sin; do not let the sun go down on your anger, and do not make room for the devil" (4:26-27).

4. What are the greatest threats or temptations that may stand in the way of my being a good husband?

Husbands who wish to do well face several worrisome threats. In a moving tape, James Dobson, of Focus on the Family, speaks of a great problem that surfaced in his marriage. After a stressful schedule of engagements, he and his wife, Shirley, found themselves in an angry confrontation concerning shared responsibilities, what each needed from the other. At the moment of confrontation, each was unable to give the other what that person needed. Dobson concludes that the most severe contemporary marriage problem is not financial crisis, fidelity, or communication but "overcommitment of our time." Having made this discovery the hard way, he goes on to describe how he restructured his life and reduced his outside commitments. He was fortunate that he was in an economic position to be able to do so.

Each of us needs to ask the same question—are we so overcommitted to work and other causes that our wives get only the dregs of us? Is it possible that we spend our time of highest energy with others and our tired hours with our spouses? If so, perhaps we also need to restructure our schedules and hear Dobson's warning.

But marriages face other hazards as well. A double-sided hazard is at once overexpectation and pessimism concerning marriage. Today, in contrast to former days, we expect so much of marriage. In days when life was a struggle for survival, couples that got the work done, provided for their families, and protected them from attack considered that they had good marriages. Now, we want a spouse who is our best friend, a glamorous, beautiful person, a magical sex partner, an equal participant in work and financial matters, our emotional intimate, our wise co-parent. And, too often, when a person scores high on many of these attributes, we fixate on the ones where she does not.

We want all these good things in a marriage, not acknowledging that for even most of these to be present, persons need to develop skills in listening, caring, handling conflict, and more. Good marriages require good people, good preparation, and constant attention and improvement. Unrealistically we want the effortless good marriage, and there is no such thing.

At the same time, there is much pessimism about marriage. Even though it is very difficult to find accurate divorce statistics—and we need to remember that the most gloomy forecasts are not true of first marriage—the worst possible divorce statistics are widely quoted. To be a good husband, I must temper my unrealistic hopes, give realistic effort, and make every effort to renew and strengthen my marriage so that I do not become a divorce statistic.

Yet another obstacle—happy problem that it is—is our increased life expectancy. We need to figure out how to renew our marriages over time so that we can survive and thrive for the long haul. Recently I stood by as a member of my congregation, ninety-one-year-old Roy Taylor, died. When Roy was twenty, he had married his sixteen-year-old sweetheart, Beulah. Their life together had contained all the struggles that the rest of us endure, and they had made it through those hardships. When it was clear that Roy's end was near, Beulah wanted so much to be able to be there to hold him, kiss him, and comfort him as he left this world. She was able to do that, completing more than seventy-one years of marriage. We husbands need to be creative in finding ways to renew our covenants and our relationships with our wives as we live through the succeeding chapters of our lives.

5. Is it ever right to give up and let go?

Is divorce ever an option for a Christian husband? Jesus strongly discouraged divorce and called us back to the one-flesh marriage. Still, his words should not become a new legalism. Rather, they are a call to make every effort to bring our marriages to a good place so that they can endure.

There will be times when there is so much pain and hurt in a marriage that divorce may be, given the circumstances, the best possible response. When that must happen, I deeply hope that the couple can come to a good place apart from each other. That good place means leaving a place for each of them in the life of any children that were born. It also means doing their best to provide for these children's growth, education, and future. I hope also that the church will not take sides, blame, or condemn the persons who decided to divorce.

Still, as one who does marriage counseling, I have the strong feeling that many couples give up too soon. Although my role as counselor requires me to help couples find their inner wisdom and direction, I sometimes find myself fighting harder for their marriage than they are. I would hope that Christian couples give a second and third effort to make a go of their marriages. Divorce may sometimes be the necessary tragic decision, but not without every exploration before that time. It is my hope that these pages contain encouragement, guidance, and tools to help each man be a better husband in the marriage where he now is.

Invitations

Some possible promises or commitments to be made:

___ to strengthen my friendship with my wife

___ to strengthen my partnership with my wife

___ to strengthen my role as lover with my wife

___ to explore with my wife how we currently manage conflict and how we might manage conflict better

___ if we are engaged in conflict, to take any steps to seek a greater reconciliation, including seeking outside help

___ if we are divorced, to seek the greatest possible respect for each other, including partnership over any children we have

___ to recommit to faithfulness to my wife

___ Write your own promises or commitments:

_____

_____

Questions for Conversation and Group Discussion

1. What do you remember most about your parents' marriage? In what ways do you want your marriage to be like theirs? In what ways do you hope it will be different?

2. What does the term *genderlect* mean? Have you had experiences in talking with members of the opposite sex that were similar to the ones described in the chapter? If so, which ones?

3. Do you think men and women have different understandings of intimacy? If so, how do they differ?

4. In your opinion, what are the greatest threats to marriage today? With each threat you list, talk about strategies to overcome it.

Resources

Dobson, James. *How to Save Your Marriage* (Life Lifters series). Waco, Tex.: Word, n.d. Audiotape.

Farrell, Warren. *The Myth of Male Power.* New York: Simon and Schuster, 1993.

Gottman, John, with Nan Silver. *Why Marriages Succeed or Fail.* New York: Simon and Schuster, 1994.

Gray, John. *Men Are from Mars; Women Are from Venus: A Practical Guide for Improving Communication and Getting What You Want in Your Relationships.* New York: HarperCollins, 1992.

Lauer, Jeanette, and Robert Lauer. "Marriages Made to Last." *Psychology Today* 19, no. 6 (June 1985): 22-26.

Levine, Beth. "How to Get Your Husband to Help at Home." *Reader's Digest,* January 1997, 183-88.

Molton, Warren Lane. *Friends, Partners, and Lovers: A Good Word about Marriage.* Valley Forge, Pa.: Judson Press, 1979.

Schmitz, Anthony. "The Secret to a Good Marriage." *Health* (March/April 1995): 51-56.

Tannen, Deborah. *You Just Don't Understand: Men and Women in Conversation.* New York: William Morrow, 1990.

Tannen, Deborah, and Robert Bly. *Men and Women: Talking Together.* New York: Sound Horizons Audio-Video, 1992. Audiotape.

Notes

1. Warren Lane Molton, *Friends, Partners, and Lovers: A Good Word about Marriage* (Valley Forge, Pa.: Judson Press, 1979).

2. John Gottman with Nan Silver, *Why Marriages Succeed or Fail* (New York: Simon and Schuster, 1994), 18, 56-66.

3. Jeanette Lauer and Robert Lauer, "Marriages Made to Last," *Psychology Today* 19, no. 6 (June 1985): 22-26.

4. Cited in Warren Farrell, *The Myth of Male Power* (New York: Simon and Schuster, 1993), 57-58.

5. Gottman with Silver, *Why Marriages Succeed or Fail,* 155.

6. Deborah Tannen, *You Just Don't Understand: Men and Women in Conversation* (New York: William Morrow, 1990).

7. John Gray, *Men Are from Mars; Women Are from Venus* (New York: Harper Collins, 1992).

8. Tannen, *You Just Don't Understand,* 49-50.

9. Ibid., 42.

10. Gray, *Men Are from Mars,* 9.

11. Tannen, *You Just Don't Understand,* 51-52.

12. Gray, *Men Are from Mars,* 60.

13. Tannen, *You Just Don't Understand,* 294.

14. Ibid., 297.

15. Anthony Schmitz, "The Secret to a Good Marriage," *Health* (March/April 1995): 56.

6

Sons and Fathers

Fathering is different from mothering. We come to our task from the outside, and captured in that configuration is the miracle we have to offer; for true fathering is not the physical act of planting a seed, it is the conscious decision to tend and nourish the seedling. Real fathering is not biological—it is the conscious choice to build an unconditional and unbreakable emotional connection to another human being.[1]

We touch the basics of a man's purpose in life when we consider a father and his child. This truth comes to us from many sources.

The Bible Teaches the Importance of Fatherhood

To begin, the Bible affirms this truth. "As a father has compassion for his children, so the LORD has compassion for those who fear Him" (Psalm 103:13). "Pray then in this way: Our Father who art in heaven . . ." (Matthew 6:9). "When we cry, 'Abba! Father!' it is that very Spirit bearing witness with our spirit that we are children of God" (Romans 8:15-16).

The Bible takes the parent-child relationship and makes it a picture for the God-human relationship. Such a stirring word picture has the reverse effect as well—it challenges us to make the God-human relationship visible by the way we relate to our children! The Bible makes clear that God entrusts tremendous power to the human relationship, and no relationship is more charged with power than that of parent-child.

The Bible uses many metaphors for God, and one of them is "father." As we note in chapter 7, another one of the Bible's metaphors for God is "mother." Without pretending that "father" is the only metaphor for God, we recognize that it is for us males a deeply powerful one.

The journey of father and child is a sacred journey. This does not mean that we are given godlike privileges or rights with our children; rather it means that we are given godlike opportunities and responsibilities with them and for them.

Our Experience Confirms the Importance of Fatherhood

In addition to the Bible's teaching, our own experience teaches us how important fatherhood is. I recall my childhood and adolescent pals and their fathers. One of my friends could count on his dad for about anything he wanted. He had the first and best bicycle, car, and so on. But he didn't see his dad much—the man was so busy being successful that there wasn't much time left for family activities. Another boy had a picture and stories of his father but not much more. His dad was a career military man who came home only occasionally. Yet another of my friends didn't know what to expect when he saw his father. If his father was drunk, he might be jolly and generous or argumentative and violent. If he was sober, he might be kind and quiet or depressed and angry. The father of another friend took great pride in his football and basketball skills. When my friend had a bad game or fouled out or lost his temper with a referee, he caught it from both the coach and his dad. Most of the boys envied me for the dad I had—he liked children, led children's groups, knew good stories and games, was a firm but fair disciplinarian. He was that way at home, too. It was great as long as it lasted.

The adult man who can say, "I received practically everything I needed from my father" is a rare and wonderfully privileged person. More often, the opposite is true. Some men are drawn to the men's movement out of a sense of loss concerning their father, and the need to explore that grief deep within. The vast majority of us who needed more of a father than we had are afflicted with a "hole in our soul," a sadness, a longing, a gnawing, and an emptiness that will not go away.

When men get together and talk, they speak of several kinds of father absence. Some types of absence inflict pain more than others, but they all hurt.

Some speak of *physically absent fathers.* These fathers may have had to work long hours or to travel for their employment. Perhaps they were in military service. Their work may have been in another city. The cultural definition of a good father in the previous few generations was that he was a good provider. Period. So if such absences made it possible for a father to provide, they were not seen as negative. And yet these very schedules may have left children without their father's attention and guidance. They still do.

Some speak of *unavailable fathers, unexpressive fathers.* These fathers could have been involved, but for some reason they were not. They did not attend and participate in their children's activities, did not praise, did not encourage, did not affirm. Many a son recalls trying to excel in something he knew interested his father (for instance, a football team). Such a son hoped for encouragement and praise from his father, but it was seldom forthcoming. These unexpressive fathers sometimes were critical of their sons' emotional expressions, particularly of tears or of fear. A grown man may remember that the last time he cried was in front of his father and that the occasion drew his father's ridicule and criticism.

Other men had *abandoning fathers.* If one's parents divorce, a child may blame himself and take on the guilt. If, for some reason, the father does not keep in touch, does not reach out, does not even remember birthdays or Christmas, the child may feel like a real failure. If a man's father has treated him that way, he may not feel good toward other men. He may feel hopeless about love (because, in his experience, love brings only pain). And he may feel incompetent about his own parenting skills. He has not seen good parenting and may not believe it is possible. Such a man may also have trouble believing in God or thinking about God.

Another form of the abandoning father is the *"deadbeat dad"*—the person who biologically sired a child but left the mother to shift for herself, providing neither emotional nor financial support. (We need to realize, of course, that harsh economic realities and a lack of skills have doomed some fathers to be "deadbeat dads." They simply couldn't provide what their families needed.)

And then some men suffered because their dads *died too young*. Samuel Osherson tells of Jose, who, though he loved his son, found himself resenting and resisting his son's request for a high school graduation party with a live band and all the trimmings. In discussing this with a friend, Jose got in touch with something connected to his feelings—his own father had died unexpectedly during his high school years. His dad had never seen him graduate from high school or college, had never seen him marry and become a father. Aware that he had missed a great deal, Jose exclaimed, "When you feel gypped yourself, it's hard to give to someone else." Once he was in touch with his own feelings and grief, Jose could rally and give his son a great party.[2]

I am one who suffered from my dad's untimely death—he died shortly before my tenth birthday, bringing a wonderful relationship to an all too abrupt, lonely, and frightening end. Decades later, I sometimes find myself overcome with sadness. I eventually went into the same profession he did. I find myself longing for one good talk with him, where we could compare experiences and swap ideas, where I could ask for his wisdom and guidance.

Some may have grown up with an *alcoholic parent*. Janet Geringer Woititz asks, "When is a child not a child?" She answers, "When a child lives with alcoholism."[3] Children need security, love, dependability. If our parents were alcoholics, the one thing we could *not* expect was dependability. Parents might be nice and loving one day, lots of fun another day, abusive and distant another day, absent another. Concern about a parent and about keeping peace with such a parent robs a child of childhood. Any reader of this book who recognizes alcoholism or another addiction in his or her own self or family is urged to take prompt steps to deal with it. Growing up under an alcoholic parent scars a person for life!

Whether we experienced our own fathers as gratifying presence or as frustrating absence, we know the significance of fatherhood.

Its Absence Is Devastating

Yet another indicator of the power of the father relationship is the devastation when it is absent. Will Glennon points out, "Nearly 80 percent of those who end up in our juvenile justice system lived in homes without a father; the overwhelming majority of our adult prison population grew up without fathers; the single strongest predictor of violent juvenile crime, specifically robbery and murder, is that the child grew up without a close relationship to his father."[4] Many urban gang members do not have a father figure and may never have known one. Indeed, membership in a gang may be seen as an effort to provide a father substitute.

Clearly, what our troubled world needs from us is the same thing that we so deeply want—that we be good fathers. But what is involved, and how do we become such persons?

What Fathers Need

If men hope to be equal to the important task of fatherhood, they need several things.

1. Fathers need healing of their own father wound. They need to deal with their own father hunger.

Studies show that men who are still angry or ambivalent about their own fathers find it difficult to be supportive

during their mate's pregnancy and delivery and find it difficult to relate to the child after birth. Each of us who feels
deprived of his father's attention, love, support, and guidance has some work to do as a prologue to parenting his
children. In some way, this truth touches all of us. As
Gabrielle Roth suggests, "It seems almost everyone grew up
without enough fathering."[5] A recent study found that only
20 percent of the fathers surveyed felt that they had an
emotionally close relationship with either their fathers or
their sons.[6] The strength of the anger and the depth of the
pain from the father hunger determine how much work we
have to do.

Some of us may find ourselves able to accept the limitations under which our fathers lived, whether external limitations like harsh economic realities or limitations within
our fathers—they just didn't know better. We may determine
that we are going to be much different fathers, but we're not
sure how. After all, we lack examples and role models. But
we're ready to muddle through and learn through experience.

Others of us may be deeply damaged by our fathers' abandonment, neglect, callousness, alcoholism, or abuse. We may
have sworn we'd never be like the old man, but to our horror,
we are coming out the same way. With shame, we recognize
we are treating our children as our fathers treated us. Then
we need more help.

Psychotherapist Alan Javurek recognizes four steps in the
inner healing that needs to take place between a man and
his destructive memories of his father. The first is awareness
of the desire for reconciliation. This could be a very subtle
inner longing to reconnect with a father from whom one has
felt distant. Or it may be a dramatic awareness that all is
not well within oneself or in important relationships.

The second is "going home," or learning more about one's
father. This learning may occur in actual visits and conversations; in studying family history, records, or photographs;
or in talking to others who know (or knew) about one's father.

It may involve an inner revisiting of childhood. New information helps us sort out who the father is as an individual.

The third step is "confronting the creative/destructive father." This involves recognizing the number of ways in which one's father has influenced one. The goal in this step is to release oneself from the father's unconscious and conscious hold. A man will probably have to face the greatest hurt and pain he experienced from his father before he can get his father in perspective and claim both the positive and negative aspects of the father. This may mean confronting physical, verbal, or sexual abuse, even if it happened in the distant past.

The fourth step is "entering into dialogue with the father." This involves an inner dialogue in which we observe and comment to ourselves about the many influences we may have internalized from our fathers. It also involves possible actual conversation with one's father.[7]

One can grow in this process even if one's father is unresponsive or takes part in only very small ways. One can grow in this process even if one's father is dead. Then the conversation is with myself and with my family history as best I can uncover it. However, I can be healed. I do not have to repeat family abuse or errors that may have persisted in my family system for centuries before I was born.

As a counselor, I have seen this happen. Quite often the reconciliation with one's father is not as the son imagined or hoped it would be. Often it is better than he feared it would be. Almost always a sense of relief and release ensues—a feeling that "Now I can get on with my life."

2. Fathers need communion, friendship, and support from other fathers and other men.

Gabrielle Roth has written,

> Communion heals the father wound. Communion with friends, lovers, parents, strangers, even enemies. But mostly with friends. Through hard trial and error and working with thousands of people, I've discovered that the heart needs to open up as fully as possible. It is a waste of time to pretend that we can't be hurt. If we're going to be

fully alive, we have to be ready to get hurt and even to hurt others. Otherwise, we're dead. Or immobilized in protective armor. In vulnerability one practices the art of friendship, the art of the heart. It is an essential spiritual practice.[8]

This sort of communion does not come easy to us men, but it is possible. We need it desperately, and once we get a vision of it, we will settle for no less. And yet a discrepancy is evident in what subjects men are willing to be vulnerable about. When we open up with each other at all, one of the first things we will discuss is our father wound. One of the last things we will discuss is any uncertainty we feel about our own parenting technique, any fear about our children's disabilities or problems, any personal failing as a parent. It seems that the old male competitiveness reappears where our own parenting is concerned. My kids are the best; my relationship with my kids is the finest. This competitiveness arises from many sources, but its deepest source is our desperate hope that we will succeed at this, life's basic purpose.

To do better with our children, we will have to quit pretending that we are doing so well. We will have to admit our uncertainties or face a tendency toward impatience, harshness, even potential abusiveness. We will need to be teachable, open. Who better to help us solve these mysteries than other fathers—older men who have been through it and peers who are working on the same issues? One of our most basic needs is communion in which we can break open our hearts about our relationships to our fathers and our children.

3. Fathers need a willingness to risk, to dance an uncertain dance.

Samuel Osherson writes beautifully about the risks of parenthood.

Fatherhood is a continual dance with uncertainty, a swaying back into the boyhood of our lives to find the responsive father within ourselves and a swing forward into the future as our growing children confront us with new issues, new aspects of ourselves. At times we have to set limits, at others lose limits; at moments we have to be "motherly" and supportive, at moments "fatherly" and affirming of mastery. Often we need to be both.

There are few simple easy answers, and often the uncertainty of being a father can be the hardest part of the experience. We wonder whether we are doing right by ourselves and our family; we wonder about our children, our parents, our own childhoods, our fitness to be parents.[9]

Parenthood is indeed an uncertain dance with all of the risks Osherson mentions. And fathers face even more risks. If a marriage feels unstable, a father is all too aware that he risks loss of the daily companionship of his children. Mothers are the primary care custodians in the vast majority of divorces. Men entering second marriages often encounter rejection from stepchildren for years (as do their spouses with theirs). And if that marriage fails, they have no visitation rights with stepchildren they may have spent years winning over.

Nevertheless, there is no other joy like the uncertain dance of fatherhood. It is well worth all the risks. The potential of the joys outweighs the risk of pain. I believe that wholeheartedly. A man needs to believe that to make a firm commitment to participate in this dance all the way through.

4. Fathers need a place to start.

Some young fathers have some advantages over us old fathers. Today's fathers are widely encouraged to be involved during pregnancy, labor, and childbirth. A large percentage of fathers are present at the birth of their children. They are among the first to hold them, to bond with them, to spend time with mother and infant. These experiences should propel them into greater involvement and greater comfort through the child's next months and years.

And yet another side exists for young fathers. Some men became fathers unwillingly—they wanted the sex but did not anticipate the pregnancy. Some feel too young or immature for fatherhood. Some find no job enabling them to support mother and child, or they have trouble coping with the day-to-day responsibilities. Fatherless children pose a grave problem for our society, and their number is growing. Some of us older fathers may be aware that we have missed out on our fathering opportunities for years. Or, at least, we have not been as involved as we now want to be. But family habits are hard to break. Whether I am a young or an old father, what can I do now?

Do something. Express an interest in a child's favorite activity. Attend a child's event. Give positive strokes whenever you can. Ask spouse and children where you can share more of their lives. The first response may not be all that you hope for. But keep at it. Father involvement and caring can enrich a child's life and may reduce the risk of that child's engaging in destructive behavior.

A man needs all of the above to empower him for his fathering role. He needs some sort of healing for his own father wound or father hunger. He needs communion, support, openness, and vulnerability with other fathers. He needs the courage to risk the ever-changing and uncertain dance of parenthood. And he needs to locate places to start changing the father-child relationships of which he has been a part.

5. Fathers need reassurance.

But fathers need one more thing—a little reassurance that what they are attempting to become as fathers is possible. If I grew up with father absence from which I haven't fully recovered, if I had abusive or addictive parents, is there any hope for me?

Yes! It may be difficult, but we are not doomed mindlessly to repeat the past. We can do several things. For one thing, we can try to understand our own father longing. Where we wanted encouragement or hugs or coaching or companionship, we can look for such opportunities to be just such a daddy for our youngsters. In those efforts may lie healing both for them and for us.

For another, we may have good parenting instincts to trust. Not all of us do, but many of us have such instincts. We may feel ourselves drawn to our children; we enjoy them and are wild about them. Those instincts, that enjoyment, that wanting the best for them will lead us to good actions and decisions as fathers.

Further, we can ask for coaching—from other men and from the children's mother. When my children were newborns, I didn't understand about talking to them and singing to them. They couldn't understand and couldn't talk back. Their mother taught me about the soothing value of the human voice. I caught on rather quickly.

If we get in touch with our love for our children and our earnest desire to be good dads, we can overcome whatever losses we had as children. Such triumphs happen frequently.

What Children Need

Just as the fulfillment of certain needs empowers us for the father task, so do our children have many things they need from us. Here is a beginning list.

1. Children need our unconditional acceptance.

To give our children unconditional acceptance and love is not as easy as it sounds. As a matter of fact, we will struggle at it and do it only partially. But struggle we must. Many, probably most, of us fathers are genuinely happy and excited to greet and hold our newborn children. And yet, rather soon, feelings enter in that complicate this welcoming attitude. These feelings may not be recognized, and if they are, they are pushed away as unworthy. Instead we have a vague sense of awkwardness and unease around our spouse and child.

I will give voice to some of those feelings with which we struggle. One goes something like this: "I married your mom because I fell in love with her and enjoyed her friendship. I still like to spend time with her and make love to her. Now you, my child, are crowding me out. I must admit a little jealousy when she cuddles you to her breast and you both enjoy it so much. Your mom and I don't go out much anymore. Nor do we have much time to talk, and when we do, it's about you. Even when we make love, she has an ear tuned to your slightest whimper. I'll try to be a good sport, but sometimes it feels like I've been replaced."

Another feeling: "I wanted a boy, but you are a girl," or vice versa. I struggled with this one myself. For our first two children, I did not care which gender—both were girls. When we were expecting our third child, which we expected to be our last, I wanted a boy more than I could admit. The baby was a girl. I loved that little girl, was loyal to her and her mother, but swallowed the disappointment. As the years went by, that little girl was such an enjoyable companion to me in so many ways. I enjoyed her tremendously. Further, one of her big sisters loved sports. She and I enjoyed many hours of softball, one-on-one basketball, and playing catch with a football. That daughter was a better athlete than I, winning many honors. My other daughter and I shared many intellectual interests and loved a good discussion. I loved and admired all three daughters—and I still do. My cup was full as the father. Nevertheless, when my first grandchild was born, and it was a boy, named after me (well, sort of, Daniel *Richard*), I felt a flood of joy beyond anything I expected.

Another of those feelings might be, "I hoped you would share my interest in sports/music/whatever, but instead you are interested in whatever/sports/music." Children will not be "chips off the old block," and we do well to affirm who they are, along with their interests.

Still another of those feelings might be, "Other children your age are walking/talking/reading/getting a job. What's the matter with you?" It is well to be in touch with caring professionals about the development of one's child. It is also good to recognize the wide variations in children's development; a child should be allowed his or her own process. Unconditional acceptance, though not easy to give, is a firm ground for our children's growth.

2. Children need our blessing.

In the Bible, we read of fathers giving their children blessings. This bestowal often occurred near the end of the father's life, as in the story of Isaac, Esau, and Jacob. In that story, Jacob (with his mother Rebekah's help) disguised himself so that he fooled his nearly blind father and stole his brother's blessing (see Genesis 27). A blessing from a father was seen as something much needed in a person's life.

In our day, to bless our children is to thank God for them, to see God's gifts in them, to ask God's guidance upon them, and to let each one know that he or she is a very special gift from God to us. Our children need our blessing throughout our lifetimes and theirs. We need to bless their existence. Why was a child born? It seems very inadequate simply to say that a man and a woman made love and a child was born. How much more complete to say that God allowed a man and woman to be partners in God's continuing creation. Here is a brand new human being, God's creation, in God's image just as I am, filled with God's potentialities. My child, I bless your birth, your existence, your life among us.

Our children need our blessing upon their efforts, their accomplishments, their milestones. Our confidence in their God-given abilities can be spoken as they face a first day in school, a first day away from home, a first day on the job, a first day of marriage.

Our children need our blessing after we have quarreled with them. They also need it when they have done wrong or when they have failed. They may need a restatement of our blessing if we have drifted apart from an earlier close communion with each other.

And when our lives draw to a close, they may need our blessing as a part of any unfinished business that lies between them and us.

3. Children need our attention to their world.

Our children need us to join them in their world. Their world has fun and laughter and games, scary dreams and other fearful things, obstacles to overcome, skills to master, disappointments, guilt. We enter their world by attending public events in which they take part, by being interested in what they are doing, by affirming and discussing with them how they felt about their participation.

We enter their world by discovering what interests them and helping them find a way to develop that interest. We enter their world by sharing activities. One-on-one activities with each child are a great good as are those that several family members can enjoy together.

Most of all, we enter their world by listening. This is a tough one for many of us fathers. We care about our children and are willing to do things for them and with them. However, listening is often not our strong suit. Still, we need to know that children's self-esteem is enhanced by adults' taking them seriously and listening to them. We need to make a studied effort on this one. Granted, we will still probably tune them out at times or drift away to thoughts of other things, but we need to look for opportunities to listen and learn. When driving a car pool, listen to the conversation among the children. When playing a game, listen to the thoughts expressed while resting between parts of the game. Ask questions—open, inquiring questions, not questions that judge or evaluate the child's performance. Our children need our attention to their world, a world made available when we listen.

4. Children need to be initiated into our world.

Fathers do not offer children some of the things that mothers do. And they offer some things that mothers do not. The following generalizations may not be true for every father, every mother, every father-mother team. However, they tend to be true.

Quite often, from early on, fathers' play with children is different from mothers' play. When fathers initiate play, it is more active, more likely to stir the child up than calm the child down; it involves more risk taking, more physical skill. This may be one gift fathers have for their children—initiation into the world they live in. For just as we need to know our children's world, they will need to learn to live in our world.

We can initiate them in many ways. We can take them along. We can invite one child to go on errands, perhaps shopping, explaining what we are looking for and how we make our choice. We can take a child to a sporting, music, or drama event we enjoy. We can bring work associates, international visitors, or other interesting people to our home. If possible, we can take our child to work. The national "Take Your Daughter to Work" day has been well received. Sons need similar exposure to the world of our work. What is there in your world with which your child will need to be familiar? Show your child your world.

5. Children need our mentoring.

We have many things to show and teach our children, things that will be extremely valuable to them. Effective, involved parenting includes numerous mentoring activities.

John Snarey conducted a detailed study on this topic and reported his discoveries in a book titled *How Fathers Care for the Next Generation.*[10] He interviewed 240 fathers about their child-rearing activities and then catalogued the variety of "generative" or "mentoring" activities of each father.

Snarey used a threefold division. The first was "social-emotional development." Examples of such activities in the "childhood decade" (a child's first ten years) include rocking a child to sleep, comforting a child afraid of the dark, taking the child to visit relatives, playing childhood games. Examples during the "adolescent decade" (the next ten years of life) include taking the child on a camping trip or to a ball game, chaperoning a dance, offering guidance on dating problems.

The second was "intellectual-academic development." Examples during the childhood decade include providing educational toys, reading to the child, playing word games, and taking the child to a library or bookstore. Examples from the adolescent decade include taking the child to a science museum, teaching a child baseball statistics, enrolling the child in special courses, discussing school courses.

The third was "physical-athletic development." Examples during the childhood decade include taking the child to the doctor, playing exercise games, or teaching the child how to swim, ride a bike, or dribble a basketball. Examples from the adolescent decade include monitoring the child's personal hygiene, teaching the child how to fish, box, throw a curve ball, or drive a car.

In my opinion, there should have been a fourth, "spiritual-moral development." The fathers interviewed included some activities in the other categories that I would include here: accompanying a child to church, arranging for religious education, participating in sex education. Other activities were not mentioned—teaching and modeling a prayer life, teaching what the parent believes is moral living, helping children with morally ambiguous decisions, involving the child in service to the world, and more.

Snarey and his research team interviewed these fathers twice, once in the childhood decade and once in the adolescent decade of their oldest child. They discovered that over the childhood and adolescent years, these fathers engaged in an average of 9.3 child-rearing activities. Father involvement varied considerably. Thirty-five percent participated in 0 to 6 child-rearing activities. Twenty-four percent were involved in 13 to more than two dozen child-rearing activities.

The researchers discovered that the fathers' involvement went down slightly as the children became older. Further, they discovered that fathers might be vitally involved in some areas but virtually absent in other aspects of the children's lives. This is regrettable, because our children need us in all areas of their lives. The extent of father involvement had vital impact on their children's lives.[11]

We never know what doors we will open for our children if we consistently make available to them what we know. Who knows what excitement we might stir, what discoveries, what dreams, if we expose them to exciting, creative, and committed people? Our children need our mentoring, our generativity.

6. Children need our spiritual-moral modeling and leadership.

Our children need from us the gift of faith. If we are to give that gift, they will need us as prayer partners, as spiritual models, as moral examples, as leaders in essential Christian practices including worship, study, and service.

Kenneth Meyering, in an interview with author Stu Weber, pointed out that when the father is an active believer, there is approximately a 75 percent likelihood that the children will also be active believers. Sadly, if the mother is a believer and the father is not, the likelihood is reduced to about 15 percent.[12]

If we want our children to be "salt of the earth" people who are supportive of the church and who work from a solid set of values, one thing we can do is more important than anything else: we can be those kinds of people ourselves! Of course, having made that commitment, we will have many other things to work out. Some fathers become so involved in church activities that their children resent their absence from the home. Other fathers may experience resistance from children—early or late—either to all religious activities or to particular ones.

Further, although we are an important influence on our children, we are not the only one. Other influences may contradict what we are trying to teach. There are no guarantees. Still, there is no single influence more powerful than the integrity of a parent's life. A sincere faith, practiced as consistently as possible; a love for Christ and church deeply felt and sacrificially lived; a desire to learn and to commune with God in worship and prayer in the company of the child; a moral code lived out as best one can—these are the things children need from us. These are some of our finest gifts.

7. Children need our discipline.

I have pointed to the need for loving atmosphere, attentive listening, and generous doses of enrichment and stimulation during childhood. But children need more. They need a consistent environment in which expectations are clear, and they need just enforcement of reasonable expectations.

As all parents know, whatever the expectation, many children will push the edges a little further, or at least try to: "I don't want to get up . . . eat quickly . . . make my bed . . .

do my chores." "You're not being fair. Why do I have to do all the work? It's not my turn to . . ."

Parents need to set the limits on that pushing. They also need to remember that the purpose of discipline is to call forth a person who will be *self*-disciplined. A good self-check for a parent during a discipline conflict is, "What does this have to do with the person I hope this child will become?" In this connection, I love the story told by a man interviewed by Will Glennon:

> My father tried to teach me how to play golf when I was about eight. For some reason, I thought I should have been able to hit the ball perfectly after a few weeks' practice. The first time he ever took me out on the course, I hit the first shot off the tee about five feet and threw my golf club about fifteen feet. That was the end of my first round of golf. Dad sat me down and told me there were three kinds of mistakes: the kind you expect—like the mis-hitting of a golf ball; the kind you make out of ignorance or inexperience— like talking when someone else is hitting, because no one ever told you that you shouldn't; and the kind you will be held responsible for because you should know better and you should be able to avoid them—like throwing your club. I was grounded for a week, but I never threw another club.[13]

I pray for that kind of wisdom in disciplining for you and for me. For our children need discipline that sets reasonable limits in the present and leads them effectively to a good place in the future.

Summary

In his workshops, Samuel Osherson often asks men to write down a gift they got from their father, something they hold dear in their hearts. Here are some of their responses:

> When I was eight years old we sat in the woods fishing. We caught some fish and cooked it over the fire. It started snowing. He pulled me between his legs, put his coat over me, and that's how we had lunch. It is the best memory of my entire life. . . .

Dad taking me with him to his chemistry lab on a Saturday morning and he and I weighing things like a strand of hair, grain of sugar, or a dot on a piece of paper on the balances in the lab. Sometimes we'd blow glass into intricate shapes. It felt good to share his work world in this way and for him to want me there. . . .

He bought a rowboat with a six-horsepower motor, so just the two of us could go fishing. . . .

Throughout childhood, sitting with my father in church, to his left. Reaching into his left-hand coat pocket for cellophane-wrapped candy. Opening the candy quietly, which was hard to do, sucking on the candy and falling asleep, leaning my head on his arm. . . .

My father helping me to learn to throw a football in a perfect spiral. . . .

I was nine years old, and it had snowed the night before. A cold, cold day, my father and I went out with our toboggan, up to the top of a sledding hill near the house. I got in first, then he, and he wrapped his coat around me for the long, windy ride down the hill. Bundled up like that, racing along, his warmth. I've never forgotten that day. . . .

A love of music. . . .

I once came upon my father when he was crying. He didn't turn away from me and he kept on crying. . . .

My father taught me my trade, with which I make my living. . . .[14]

In our interactions with our children, who knows when that moment will happen that will be remembered forever, that will influence a lifetime? Such opportunities come to us who lovingly persist in our fathering task.

What Our Sons Need

In addition to those things that all children need, are there things that our sons specifically need of us? Yes, a few.

1. Sons need male energy and any skills or interests the father can offer.

Robert Bly has sensed something very destructive happening to the father-son relationship in our culture. He writes, "Only one hundred and forty years have passed since factory work began in the West, and we see in each generation poorer bonding between father and son, with catastrophic results." The legacy of that industrial era has remained with us: "the father was working but the son could not see him working."[15]

A strong cultural-economic trend has changed the way fathers and children, particularly sons, relate. They have less contact. Bly notes, "When a father, absent during the day, returns home at six, his children receive only his temperament, and not his teaching."[16] This may be a fatigued and touchy temperament. The son spends less time with his father, absorbs less, learns less. At the same time, misunderstandings and suspicions between them can grow. Bly contends that fathers seem to get smaller in each succeeding generation.

Fortunately, counteracting forces are at work today—a larger emphasis on the importance of fatherhood, a variety of working schedules, a growth of home industries, to mention a few. How important that we take advantage of these trends and be more available to our children.

A father offers his sons something different from what a mother offers. Bly speaks of male energy, male juices, male rhythms. We have absorbed female energy, juices, and rhythms from being in the womb close to the mother's heartbeat, being close to her in infancy, feeding at her breast. A wise father spends much time with his son, so that his son can become "tuned" to the father's inner melody and rhythms as well. In yet another way, Bly suggests, "When a father and son do spend long hours together, which some fathers and sons still do, we could say that a substance almost like food passes from the older body to the younger."[17]

Granted, this gift is more vague than some of the other opportunities for fathers, but it is real. It consists primarily of inviting our sons to spend time with us in our work, our chores, our play, our interests. Quite likely our sons will pick up on some of these and not on others. That's OK and is preferable to our sons' missing out on interests or opportunities that no one ever showed them.

2. Sons need sensitivity and support during some of the harsh experiences of male children.

We consider below some of the harsh ways our culture treats girls. Michael Gurian points out that each gender has equally painful sufferings. As fathers, we are wise to be alert and sensitive so that we can support our sons when they may be hurting. Studies show that parents tend to talk to, cuddle, and breast-feed boy infants less than girl infants. Male babies have a 25 percent higher mortality rate. They are twice as likely to suffer from autism and learning disabilities, six times as likely to be diagnosed with hyperkinesis. The majority of schizophrenic and mentally retarded children are boys. Emotionally disturbed boys outnumber girls four to one.

Twice as many boys as girls are injured and die from physical abuse. Unless we learn to model a different way of handling emotions, many boys will have learned by age nine to repress all feelings except anger. Rage then becomes the way that repressed pain, fear, sadness, and grief are expressed. When this is the pattern, boys are violent with each other. Thus boys are three times as likely as girls to be the victims of violence (even when rape and incest are included in the statistics). Gurian points out that today an African American boy in an urban area is more at risk of dying of a gunshot wound than was an African American male in the Vietnam War. Or boys may turn the rage on themselves—they are four times as likely as girls to commit suicide.

What's going on in all these grim scenarios? Boys are showing their desperate need for caring, for male-sensitive parenting, supported by the surrounding community. A mother once asked Gurian, "In twenty-five words or less, what does a boy need?" The group he was leading came up with the following answers: "(1) nurturing parents/caregivers, (2) a clan or tribe, (3) spiritual life, (4) important work, (5) mentors and role models, (6) to know the rules, (7) to learn how to lead, how to follow, (8) an adventure, and a best friend to have it with, (9) lots of games, (10) an important role in life."[18] In other words, they need male-sensitive parenting.

3. Sons need the joy of male companionship.

I was once awaiting the arrival of a close friend, Lee (of whom I spoke in chapter 4), who was to lead an event at my church. My oldest daughter, Julie, then a teenager, asked if she could meet Lee at the airport with me as she had done on his previous visit. I wasn't sure, because his flight arrival was uncertain, and so I asked her why she wanted to go. "Because you guys are nuts!" she responded. I invited her to go. I have always been grateful that she experienced how much fun I had with that particular friend, who is now dead. When her son, Daniel, visits me, I want him to meet and enjoy my friends, the ways we spend time together, the jokes and kidding and humor we share with each other.

Wherever we find our male bonding, we are wise to invite our sons to be part of it. Outdoor activities, organized sports (whether participating or watching), hanging out, or whatever puts us in touch with the men we enjoy—how good it is if, at least occasionally, our sons can be a part. We want them to know that we enjoy being male, that we have good friends we count on, and that perhaps there will be a time when they will want to talk to some of our friends.

4. Sons need help in initiation and separation.

As we noted in chapter 2, some writers on male issues make much of the fact that earlier cultures had initiation rites for young males coming of age. These were conducted by the older men of the tribe to introduce a child into a world that is "not mother." After that rite, he would relate to both his parents in a different way. He became a man.

I am not so sure we need an initiation ceremony. But we do need to help our sons be free. They will need to be free from too close parental ties (not just maternal ties) so that they are prepared to form loving relationships and establish their own families. They will need to be made free by good work habits, the ability to care for themselves (to feed and clothe themselves), employment skills, and healthy attitudes so that they can make their way. They will need to be free to discover what they believe and what ideals they will serve. Both parents will have a part in this preparation. It may be that as the mother had unique gifts to offer at the son's arriving, the father may have unique gifts to offer at his launching. At important times (being baptized, being confirmed, getting the first car or the first job, graduating, leaving home, getting married) a father will be wise to spend time with a son. The accomplishment can be celebrated; goodbyes can be said; the child can be assured that the next step is achievable. And a father, sharing in these times, can learn to let go.

What Our Daughters Need

Quite probably, our daughters need some things from us that are quite different from what our sons need. Here are at least a few:

1. Daughters need communion with and affirmation from the opposite sex.

Charles Scull notes,

A father is the first and often the longest connection a daughter will have with a man. The father-daughter bond (or lack of bond) shapes her future relationships with male friends and lovers and influences how she moves out in the world.

If he encourages her efforts to achieve, inspires her budding self-confidence, and teaches her competency skills, she will more easily develop an authentic self-esteem. If he discourages her efforts, undermines her self-confidence, shames her body, or discounts her personal opinions, her self-esteem will be marred, and it may take many years for her to learn to believe in herself.[19]

For many a father in those early years of parenthood, nothing is easier than loving, caring for, protecting, a little girl who adores him. I remember how much I enjoyed my daughters in their infancy, preschool years, early school years. Tearful goodbyes in the morning, exuberant welcomes when I came home from work, delight in the simplest game, walk, or park outing together—what memories those are! I thought my daughters were wonderful, and they returned the compliment.

However, little girls grow and change, and wise fathers must change the way they relate to them. William Appleton suggests three stages of father-daughter interaction: *oasis,* the time the daughter is in childhood; *conflict,* during the adolescent years; and *separation,* as she becomes an adult.[20] This progression is complicated by the fact that the little girl becomes a young woman. As a daughter's menstruation begins and her bodily form develops, her father may be confused about a fitting father-daughter style. One woman recalls that she and her father were playfully affectionate— she would sit on his lap, kiss him often, and hug or dance with him. As she entered her teen years, her father pulled back. She missed this happy time and wondered what she had done wrong.

Before my daughters reached this point, I was told of a custom that I decided to adopt. This custom was that at a daughter's first menstruation, the father sent her roses. Each time, my wife informed me, and each time I sent roses with a personal note, delivered by the florist. In that way, I hoped to be a part of this time of growth and passage in my daughters' lives. One daughter put it in perspective. After the flowers arrived and she thanked me, she added, "Dad, since I'm on the 'dawn of womanhood' [a phrase from my note], can I have a raise in my allowance?"

I read of another father who did much better. He created a rite of passage for each of his daughters shortly after a first period. He and that daughter did something they had long enjoyed—they camped out for a night. They sat and talked; he affirmed her, her life, her growth and change, her relationships, her future, and more. He gave each daughter a significant gift to remember the time. He looked back on these times as something that he and his daughters treasure.[21]

Even with such a good beginning, father and daughter may not know just how to relate to each other in her teen years. Both may have changeable feelings, confused feelings at times. A woman remembers pushing away her father's hug when she was twelve. She said she got a message from him in response, "I'll never hug you again," and he didn't. She remembers that her feelings changed from time to time, and in refusing that hug, she was not making a once-and-for-all statement!

Tom Dunn, one of my counseling mentors, shared with me a view on all this that made sense. He suggested that a father needs a delicate balance between two strong feelings and that either strong feeling by itself is unhealthy. On the one hand, the father needs an attitude of commitment to the safety and privacy of his daughter. On the other hand, the father needs to delight in the emerging woman that is his daughter with feelings of enthusiasm, warmth, attraction. If the father overemphasizes the first feeling without the second, he is cold, withdrawn, remote. If the father over-emphasizes the second feeling without the first, he may behave inappropriately, flirting or coming dangerously close to violating incest barriers. Those two attitudes in healthy tension will serve father and daughter well. Out of this there may be a communion between the two that survives and remains strong during growth and change.

2. Daughters need support to help them survive the pressures of adolescence.

In her powerfully compassionate and insightful book *Reviving Ophelia: Saving the Selves of Adolescent Girls,* Mary Pipher suggests that "adolescent girls are saplings in a hurricane."[22] At least three factors make girls vulnerable to the hurricane. First, as we have noted, on their developmental level, everything is changing, including body shape, hormones, skin, hair. This in turn stirs that most basic question, "What is my place in the universe; what is my meaning?"

Second, she points out that American culture has always been hard on girls in early adolescence. Here they will experience, with a fierceness they have not faced before, damaging "isms"—sexism, capitalism, and lookism (the evaluation of a person solely on appearance).

Third, these girls are expected to separate from parents just at the time they most need their parents' support. There is more at stake here than simply the question of how a father and daughter ought to relate.[23] The issue of whether the adolescent girl will have a firm base of support and wisdom, and whether she will trust it, is even more pressing.

Though these things have always been true, Pipher detects an ever harsher cultural environment for early adolescent girls today. She says it is more difficult for girls today than it was for her in her girlhood thirty years ago, and even harsher today than ten years ago. She writes,

> Many of the pressures girls have always faced are intensified in the 1990s. Many things contribute to this intensification: more divorced families, chemical addictions, casual sex and violence against women. Because of the media, which Clarence Page calls "electronic wallpaper," girls all live in one big town—a sleazy, dangerous tinsel town with lots of liquor stores and few protected spaces. Increasingly women have been sexualized and objectified, their bodies marketed to sell tractors and toothpaste. Soft- and hard-core pornography are everywhere. Sexual and physical assaults on girls are at an all-time high. Now girls are more vulnerable and fearful, more likely to have been traumatized and less free to roam about alone. This combination of old stresses and new is poison for our young women.[24]

Pipher, for example, was in college before she had to face the issues of premarital sex, alcohol, and drugs. Now many girls ages ten to thirteen are having to face those same decisions!

Although it would be nice if this harsh youth culture would change, certain things are needed in the meantime. Pipher calls for homes that help girls hold on to their true selves, that offer girls both protection and challenges, that give girls affection and structure. In such homes girls hear the message "I love you, but I have expectations." Girls need homes where parents set firm guidelines and communicate high hopes. It is hoped that if such a base is formed in

childhood, love and respect for parents will persist through
the teen years. For this to occur, fathers and mothers need to
build alliances of mutual respect and support. They may
well need each other in some of the storms of the adolescent
hurricane. They may need to be a "tag team" alternating in
offering support and firm discipline.

3. Daughters need our belief in them and our support
beyond gender stereotypes.

Our daughters need our support and acceptance in the
present. They are also influenced by our view of their future.
Each of us needs to ask what kind of future we want for our
daughters. Do we want them to use any talent or gift they
have, pursue any occupation that draws them and uses their
best? Or do we place limitations on what is appropriate for
their life course? I suspect that most of us want our daughters to pursue any dream that beckons. If so, we need to
communicate this desire clearly.

For example, Marjorie Lozoff, after a four-year study of
women's career success, concluded that the women who were
most self-determining had fathers who "treated the daughters as if they were interesting people, worthy and deserving
of respect and encouragement." Women starting from such a
base "did not feel their femininity was endangered by the
development of talent." These were women whose fathers
had invited and encouraged their daughters to take an active interest in their own professional lives as well as in such
interests as politics, sports, or the arts.[25]

There is evidence that even though many fields are more
open to women now than in the past, some girls still believe
the fields are too difficult for them. These are fields in which
few women role models, mentors, professors, or peers exist.
Some specialized fields in engineering would be examples.
A father can be supportive of the daughter who is feeling
this type of loneliness. Belief in the daughter and curiosity
and openness to her chosen world of work can ease the
loneliness. Our commitment to encouraging our daughter's
ability and helping to shape a world that is open to her
talents is a most important gift to give.

Fathering without Custody or without Biological Children

So far we have talked mainly about parenting where both parents can be present to their children daily. That is far from the reality of many children and many fathers. Many children do not have a father and mother in residence. Through no fault of their own, these children are in quite different circumstances. They may be orphans, children of divorce or desertion, offspring of an unwed mother. Or they may be children or youths whose families gave up on them, and thus they are placed in a foster home or a group home for children. As much as any child—and perhaps even more—these children need a caring adult male in their lives.

I was one of those children from the age of nine, when my dad died. At the time, I don't think I knew what I needed or wanted. I hoped that my mother would not remarry, because I felt that no one could take my dad's place (she didn't). If any man offered extra attention, care, help, or mentoring to me, I didn't notice it, or I pushed it away. At the same time, I didn't know how to do many of the things that boys learn from men—hunting, fishing, fixing things, horseback riding, driving, to mention a few. There were some things I wished I knew, but I never even thought of talking them over with a man, because I didn't feel close enough to any man. These included things like how to be popular with girls, how to understand them, how to treat them, how far to go.

It strikes me now, as I look back, that no man reached out to this lonely, unsure-of-himself boy—no teacher, coach, employer, man at church. I must hasten to add that I was among the lucky fatherless boys. My mother and her two close woman friends gave close attention to parenting me, teaching me good work skills, recognizing and encouraging my gifts.

Though very poor, my mother made it clear that we would sacrifice so that I could go to college and get training to be whatever I wanted. So that part of my education was fine. As I look back with today's consciousness and insights, I see a gap that, had it been filled, would have made me a happier, more confident child and youth. Nonetheless, I trust that I am a living testimony that fatherless boys can grow up and do quite well in this world.

I hope that my childhood experience makes me more sensitive to the needs of children around me today. May I see the boys and girls who need some of the same things I needed and be there for them. And may you offer what you have to give.

Some of us may be divorced fathers without custody. Such a father may have scheduled occasions to visit the child or bring the child to his home. Fathers in this circumstance tell me that theirs is a tough duty. It may feel unnatural and awkward—and it may be hard to keep motivated to persist in these contacts. Or these times may bring such joy and closeness that it tears both father and child apart to have to say goodbye. Geographical moves may make it difficult to have much contact at all.

A father thus shut out has an understandable grief and frustration to work out. He knows pain in wanting to be important in a child's life and feeling unable to do it. It is important that a father feel that grief and then resolve to do all that he can. Too often children, who did not cause the divorce, bear the greatest scars from it. Parents can resolve that they will do everything they can to minimize the scars.

For a father, it will mean making every contact he can—perhaps in person, perhaps by phone or by mail. Special days should be remembered consistently. One father, aware of his son's love of computers, learned how to communicate with him using e-mail. It will also mean managing conflict with the children's mother and not letting the children feel the strain of any residual anger. It may even mean helping the children accept and learn from a new stepfather if the children's mother remarries. It may mean exploring the possibility of a healing reconciliation if the mother has not remarried.

Samuel Osherson has noted that a recent survey of father-child contact after a divorce showed that by early adolescence,

50 percent of the children had no contact with their fathers, 30 percent had sporadic contact, and only 20 percent of the children saw their fathers once a week or more. He adds, "We may be facing a psychological time bomb within the younger generations of men and women now coming of age."[26] May the number of divorced fathers who give their children continuing attention and care increase!

However, try as he might, that nonresidential, noncustodial father cannot be there each time his children need such a presence, and that is where some of the others of us may enter in. We need a pattern of being available and helpful with each other's children.

Robert Bly has pointed out that in times past, the term *grandfather* was not a term to describe a biological relationship. It simply meant "old father." The old fathers of a village had a role in welcoming, initiating, guiding the young of the community. And Wallace Charles Smith has pointed out how the sibling-based family structure of West Africa persists among many African Americans. They create extended family relationships, perhaps with persons not biologically or legally related. Those possessing this heritage may have many male models participating in the life of the children.[27]

And so there is a place for each of us, whether our children are old or young, whether we live in the community where our children are or farther away, indeed whether we have any biological children or not. For as Will Glennon told us at the beginning of this chapter, "true fathering is not the physical act of planting a seed, it is the conscious decision to tend and nourish the seedling."

Invitations

As you reflect on your parenting task, you may want to make some of these commitments:

    __ to teach your child something about a hobby or sport that you enjoy

    __ to listen to your children more

___ to find ways to express interest in children who are not your biological children but who may need a little extra male attention

___ to be a spiritual example and guide to your children

___ if you are a divorced father, to make every effort to keep contact with your children, letting them know how important they are to you

___ Write your own:

Questions for Conversation and Group Discussion

1. What are your happiest memories of your father? What are the gifts—of self, of achievement, of interest—that you received from your father?

2. Do you feel you have a "father wound"? What did you need from your father that you did not receive? What sort of father absence did you experience, if any?

3. What do you most enjoy with your children? What do your children most enjoy with you?

4. About what aspects of fathering do you feel puzzled or discouraged? On what topics would you like to hear the experience and wisdom of other fathers?

Resources

Fields, Suzanne. *Like Father, Like Daughter: How Father Shapes the Woman His Daughter Becomes.* Boston: Little, Brown, 1983.

Glennon, Will. *Fathering: Strengthening Connection with Your Children No Matter Where You Are.* Berkeley, Calif.: Conari Press, 1995.

Greenberg, Martin. *Birth of a Father.* New York: Continuum, 1985.

Gurian, Michael. *The Wonder of Boys: What Parents, Mentors, and Educators Can Do to Shape Boys into Exceptional Men.* New York: Jeremy P. Tarcher/Putnam Book, 1996.

Lamott, Anne. *Operating Instructions.* Avemal, N.J.: Random House, 1993.

Osherson, Samuel. *The Passions of Fatherhood.* New York: Fawcett Columbine, 1995.

———. "The Wounded Father Within." In *Fathers, Sons, and Daughters: Exploring Fatherhood, Renewing the Bond,* ed. Charles Scull, 241-46. Los Angeles: Jeremy P. Tarcher, 1992.

———. *Wrestling with Love: How Men Struggle with Intimacy with Women, Children, Parents, and Each Other.* New York: Fawcett Columbine, 1992.

Pipher, Mary. *Reviving Ophelia: Saving the Selves of Adolescent Girls.* New York: Ballantine Books, 1994.

Pruett, Kyle. *The Nurturing Father: Journey toward the Complete Man.* New York: Warner Books, 1987.

Schnur, Steven. *Daddy's Home! Reflections of a Family Man.* New York: Crown, 1990.

Scull, Charles, ed. *Fathers, Sons, and Daughters: Exploring Fatherhood, Renewing the Bond.* Los Angeles: Jeremy P. Tarcher, 1992.

Secunda, Victoria. *Women and Their Fathers: The Sexual and Romantic Impact of the First Man in Your Life.* New York: Delacorte Press, 1992.

Smith, Wallace Charles. *The Church in the Life of the Black Family.* Valley Forge, Pa.: Judson Press, 1985.

Snarey, John. *How Fathers Care for the Next Generation: A Four Decade Study.* Cambridge, Mass.: Harvard University Press, 1993.

Weber, Stu. *Tender Warrior: God's Intention for a Man.* Sisters, Oreg.: Multnomah Books, Questar, 1993.

Woititz, Janet Geringer. *Adult Children of Alcoholics.* Deerfield Beach, Fla.: Health Communications, 1983.

Notes

1. Will Glennon, *Fathering: Strengthening Connections with Your Children No Matter Where You Are* (Berkeley, Calif.: Conari Press, 1995), 215.

2. Samuel Osherson, *Wrestling with Love: How Men Struggle with Intimacy with Women, Children, Parents, and Each Other* (New York: Fawcett Columbine, 1992), 80.

3. Janet Geringer Woititz, *Adult Children of Alcoholics* (Deerfield Beach, Fla.: Health Communications, 1983).

4. Glennon, *Fathering*, 5.

5. Gabrielle Roth, "Befriending Your Father," cited in *Fathers, Sons, and Daughters: Exploring Fatherhood, Renewing the Bond*, ed. Charles Scull (Los Angeles: Jeremy P. Tarcher, 1992), 215.

6. Glennon, *Fathering*, 2.

7. Alan Javurek, "Midlife Reconciliation with the Father," cited in *Fathers, Sons, and Daughters*, ed. Scull, 223-29.

8. Roth, cited in *Fathers, Sons, and Daughters*, ed. Scull, 216.

9. Osherson, *Wrestling with Love*, 243.

10. John Snarey, *How Fathers Care for the Next Generation: A Four-Decade Study* (Cambridge, Mass.: Harvard University Press, 1993).

11. Ibid., 32-54.

12. Stu Weber, *Tender Warrior: God's Intention for a Man* (Sisters, Oreg.: Multnomah Books, Questar, 1993), 132.

13. Glennon, *Fathering*, 170.

14. Osherson, *Wrestling with Love*, 64-65, 306-7.

15. Robert Bly, "The Hunger for the King in a Time with No Father," in *Fathers, Sons, and Daughters*, ed. Scull, 62.

16. Ibid., 64.

17. Ibid., 61.

18. Michael Gurian, *The Wonder of Boys: What Parents, Mentors, and Educators Can Do to Shape Boys into Exceptional Men* (New York: Jeremy P. Tarcher/Putnam Book, 1996), xvii-xxi.

19. Scull, *Fathers, Sons, and Daughters*, 99.

20. William Appleton, cited ibid., 101.

21. Tom Pinkson, "Honoring a Daughter's Emergence into Womanhood," cited ibid., 149-54.

22. Mary Pipher, *Reviving Ophelia: Saving the Selves of Adolescent Girls* (New York: Ballantine Books, 1994), 22.

23. Ibid., 22-23.

24. Ibid., 27-28.

25. Marjorie Lozoff, cited in Maureen Murdock, "Daughters in the Father's World," in *Fathers, Sons, and Daughters*, ed. Scull, 108.

26. Samuel Osherson, "The Wounded Father Within," in *Fathers, Sons, and Daughters*, ed. Scull, 242.

27. Wallace Charles Smith, *The Church in the Life of the Black Family* (Valley Forge, Pa.: Judson Press, 1985).

7

Faith

Let's pause for a moment of reflection. We have looked at men's movements and at the present-day search for the male role and soul. Then we went on to consider four key concerns for men—emotions and stress management; friendships and groups; marriage and relationships with women; and being sons and fathers.

It is now time for our exploration to turn in a different direction. It is time to ask directly: how do we state a faith perspective that is big enough for us men today? What is a man's Christian calling for such a time as this? In this chapter we will look at faith; in the next, at calling. Here I address those aspects of the Christian faith that speak especially to men and also the ways that men can relate to our biblical heritage. I also discuss gender-related faith issues that are important for men to consider.

Yet I almost despair before beginning. How can I speak of the vastness of the faith to the incredible variety of men who may read this?

Though I have discussed these topics with many men, all I can give you is a personal statement, a testimony. Here is where I stand—here is what speaks powerfully out of the Christian faith to me. From what I have heard, here is my report about how men make this their own. Here also are a few ways to stretch your souls in your faith journeys.

Jesus as Lord, Savior, Pioneer, and Friend

At the foundation is our faith in Jesus as Lord, Savior, Pioneer, and Friend. He is our *Lord,* the one to whom we are accountable, the one whom we long to be like, the one whose example we try to follow.

Generations ago, Charles Sheldon wrote a stirring, searching novel, *In His Steps.* He told the story of a minister who preaches on 1 Peter 2:21, "For to this you have been called, because Christ also suffered for you, leaving you an example, so that you should follow in his steps." Then in his failing to respond to a needy person, the pastor awakes to how far he is from following in Jesus' steps. He resolves to do so and invites persons in his congregation to do likewise. The rest of the novel is the imaginative story of the striking changes and revolutions that occur when people conduct their lives and work asking, "What would Jesus do?"[1]

Men in each generation need to ask this question anew—what would it look like to follow in his steps? As we seek a faithful way for living as males, there are so many ways in which we can simply follow "in his steps":

in the freedom of his emotions—from tears to laughter, from tenderness to anger

in his reaching out for the friendship and support of others

in his respect, trust, and high regard for women

in his love and concern for children and their families

in his inspiring prayer life that gave him power to endure all he had to face

in his purposefulness in discovering and following that for which he had come into the world

in the way his presence was a means of listening, caring, and healing folks

in his willingness to sacrifice, to give his life for his friends

Jesus is our Lord. He is also our Lord in that his purpose for the world is our purpose. He wants the world to be won and people to be discipled. Each of us is to find a way to be obedient to our Lord.

Jesus is also our *Savior,* the bringer of salvation. That word, *salvation,* means deliverance from that which would enslave us; it also means health in all its dimensions. Jesus is our deliverer and our bringer of health. He delivers us from shame, including the shame we sometimes feel in being men. He delivers us from embarrassment about not being the kind of men that society expects us to be. He also delivers us from our fear, our timidity, our shyness that keeps us from being the men we feel called to be. He loves us and accepts us as we are, though we are morally imperfect. He forgives us and saves us from our sins.

He empowers us to battle our moral hang-ups, our unhealthy habits, our addictions. He is with us in our failures and our triumphs. He persists with us though we fail time and time again.

Jesus is our Savior—our deliverer and healer.

Although Savior and Lord are two widely accepted ways to think of Jesus, a third word is helpful for us men seeking to find our way. This word, though used only four times in the New Testament, has great significance: the Greek term *archegos.* The term can mean several related things—founder, source, origin, or, perhaps more accurately, *pioneer.* William Barclay suggests, "An *archegos* is someone who begins something in order that others may enter into it. . . . An *archegos* is one who blazes the trail for others to follow."[2]

The term *archegos* is used in Acts 3:15—"the author [pioneer] of life"; in Acts 5:31—"our leader [pioneer] and savior"; in Hebrews 2:10—"the pioneer of [our] salvation"; and in Hebrews 12:2—"the pioneer and perfecter of our faith." These verses describe Jesus as pioneer of life, salvation, and faith. This means that Jesus is not only important for what he did on our behalf, or for the things he did that we should imitate. He is also important because he pointed us in new directions. He sets us free to follow his pioneering and to become pioneers as well. There is new territory to discover; there are new trails to blaze. In this we follow the leading of the one who is pioneer and calls us to be pioneers for a new and different age.

In his book *Tender Warrior,* Stu Weber finds an image of men's calling in Flint MacCullugh, from the old TV series *Wagon Train.* You may recall that MacCullugh was the scout who rode ahead to see what needed to be faced, what problems and emergencies to anticipate. In Weber's words, Flint was a *provisionary:*

> Looking ahead. Giving direction. Anticipating needs. Defining the destination. Riding ahead of the wagon on scout duty.
>   What makes a man? First, foremost, and above all else, it is *vision.* A vision for something larger than himself. A vision of something out there ahead. A vision of a place to go. A cause to give oneself for. Call it a sense of destiny. Call it a hill to climb. A mountain to conquer. A continent to cross. A dream glimmering way out there on the horizon. Call it what you will, but at its heart, it's vision. A man must visualize ahead of time. Project. Think forward. Lift his eyes and chart the course ahead. Ask leading questions. Picture the future. Anticipate what the months and years may bring. A provisionary is one who lives at and beyond the horizons.[3]

Weber's terms *scout* and *provisionary* are very close to what I mean by pioneer. Jesus is our Lord, Savior, and Pioneer, who makes us pioneers as well and who sends us out on a journey of discovery. These discoveries are both for ourselves and for others.

Jesus Christ, the One from God, is one thing more. He is our *Friend.* The Gospels portray Jesus as a loyal, loving friend and as one who reached out asking for friendship for himself. He chose an inner group of twelve "to be with him" (Mark 3:14). He shared vital experiences with his friends and asked for their support in prayer when his heart was "sorrowful unto death." He called them friends and told them that—as good friends do—he had revealed all that he had to tell them (John 15:13-15).

In John 1 we are told, "the Word became flesh and lived among us, . . . full of grace and truth" (v. 14). Jesus is the enfleshed one, a person from God who has shared life in all its dimensions with us. Thus we dare claim that the friend of those on the Gospel pages is also our friend! Friends support, sustain, understand, forgive, and encourage. Jesus is that kind of friend to each of us.

Jesus as Lord, Savior, Pioneer, and Friend—each of these words interprets and influences the others. That is where my faith journey begins.

A Pair of Recognitions

I believe that in our journey of faith, we need to recognize two things. These are freeing both for us and for others.

Spiritual Gifts for Both Genders

One recognition is that God entrusts gifts to all people and to both genders. Take, for example, the gifts and calling that lead one to be a minister of the gospel. We need to be aware and supportive of the truth that God calls and gives spiritual gifts to both men and women.

It is unfortunate that a misreading and overemphasis of a few Bible verses lead some to think that women should not be ordained ministers. It is even more unfortunate that we have missed the several Gospel references that show that Jesus was ministered to by women in many ways. (See Luke 8:1-3; 10:38-42; 7:36-50; 23:55-24:11.) Further, the New Testament shows that women were in places of significant pastoral leadership in the New Testament church. (See Romans 16, where Phoebe is called a deacon [minister] and benefactor. Also mentioned are Prisca, a co-worker; Mary, a hard worker; and Junia, an apostle.) If only we had had a more balanced reading and interpretation of these passages for generations—for centuries! We might have spared ourselves countless arguments. We also might have not broken the hearts of many who felt the stirrings of ministry but were told it was not for them.

I believe that Scripture affirms the gifts and calling of both men and women. Further, a new force is stirring and moving among us. The Spirit is moving, calling women in large numbers to ministry. In many seminaries these days, half or more of the student body consists of women. This is true both in the United States and in several seminaries in Asia that I visited recently.

However, a sad thing too often happens. A woman discerns that God is calling her to ministry. Her home church affirms this call and licenses her. She completes theological school, having done excellent work. And then no church calls her! Well-meaning Christians resist out of misunderstanding of Scripture and out of tradition. Some have claimed that if a woman is pastor, the church will lose its men. I hope that men with pro-vision will be open to their church's calling of a qualified woman pastor and that these men will be open to receive her ministry. I call men to be open and affirming even when some women in the congregation are not. Perhaps this is part of the pioneering to which we are called, to support these talented women pastors.

In turn, they may well surprise us with their many gifts, creativity, and vision. These pastors may be God's means of bringing renewal and revival to our churches. I know whereof I speak. My mentor in ministry from the time I was ten was a woman minister—my home pastor. Her dedicated service won over a skeptical Western town and called back to life a tiny, nearly dead congregation. Women ministers before and after her have been similarly used by God.

But ordained ministry is only one area where we need greater freedom about God's spiritual gifts to us. We need to shake loose from what we think are typically men's gifts and what are typically women's gifts. Take, for example, the care of small children. When I retire shortly, I hope to take regular turns in the nursery, setting a young mother free to spend an hour in the presence of adults worshipping and growing spiritually. I will be willing to prepare the Communion beforehand and clean up afterward—letting the women serve at the worship celebration. I will "remember" how to run the dishwasher (similar to the one I ran to earn my way through school). Then I'll volunteer for some of that work and invite women who often prepare the food and do the dishes for us to go out, sit down, and enjoy the program. If I am on the nominating committee, I will advocate that women with administrative and financial skills be used in places that often have been only male territory in churches. These are but a few examples of claiming gifts and breaking free.

Language about God

The other recognition concerns how we think of God and the language we use in speaking of God. Most frequently we speak of God by using metaphors or similes. As we remember from English class, metaphors and similes are words that compare one entity to another. Since we cannot fathom the nature of the eternal God, we choose terms from human experience to help us understand some aspect or characteristic of God. Each metaphor or simile opens up something about God we would not have otherwise discovered.

The Bible uses many metaphors for God. Further, the Bible contains firm prohibitions against idolatry, the substitution of anything for God as the object of worship. And so to absolutize any one metaphor about God, making that word or phrase *the* description of God, is idolatry. We are much wiser and more obedient if we follow the Bible in using many metaphors about God, letting each one, and all of them in concert, point to the reality of the divine.

Bible writers use masculine, feminine, and gender-neutral metaphors and similes for God. Some of the gender-neutral similes suggest that God is like a wall, a shield, a fortress, a rock, a sword, a word, glory (that is, light), the morning dew. Although these images offer a moment of insight or reflection, they stir no great excitement, emotion, or identification.

The Bible also uses feminine metaphors for God. It portrays God as *mother,* as one who gives birth:

"you forgot the God who gave you birth" (Deuteronomy 32:18; see also Isaiah 42:14). God also provides the traditional motherly nurturing:

When Israel was a child, I loved him,
    and out of Egypt I called my son. . . .
Yet it was I who taught Ephraim to walk,
    I took them up in my arms;
    but they did not know that I healed them.
                                —Hosea 11:1, 3

As a mother comforts her child,
    so I will comfort you.
                                —Isaiah 66:13

Can a woman forget her nursing child,
    or show no compassion for the child of her womb?
Even these may forget,
    yet I will not forget you.
                                —Isaiah 49:15

The Bible portrays God as *midwife* and *nursemaid* (Isaiah 46:3-4; Psalm 22:9; Isaiah 66:9). God is portrayed as performing such culturally assigned "womanly" tasks as providing food for the children of Israel in the wilderness (Exodus 16) and of clothing both Adam and Eve and the children of Israel (Genesis 3:21). Further, there are Bible images and terms that those who read the Bible in the original languages would recognize as female metaphors. Somehow these have been lost in translation. For example, the word for womb or uterus in Hebrew is *rehem*. The plural of *rehem* is *rehemim*, which usually means not "wombs" but rather the abstract qualities of compassion, mercy, and love. In the Bible, then, compassion is "womb-love," or mother love, the love of a woman for the one whom she has born. In Jeremiah 31:20, God says,

Is Ephraim my dear son?
    Is he the child I delight in?
As often as I speak against him,
    I still remember him.
Therefore I am deeply moved for him;
    I will surely have mercy on him, says the Lord.

In this passage the term *mercy* in the last line is literally motherly compassion, "womb-love." (See also Psalm 71:6 and Isaiah 49:1.)

There are other terms for God or about God that ancient Hebrew readers would have recognized as feminine in gender: *hokmah*—wisdom, which in Proverbs 8 danced before God and was the enabling power at creation; *Torah*—God's teaching, law, instruction; *shekinah*—the glory of God, God's presence manifest on earth; and *ruach,* spirit or wind. Spirit is considered feminine in Hebrew, the language of the Old Testament, and neuter in Greek, the language of the New Testament. Speakers often refer to the Holy Spirit as "he." They would be more accurate if they described the Holy Spirit as "she" or "it." Granted, these feminine metaphors and images for God are not frequent in the Bible. But that they are present at all in a book written in a male-dominated culture is a witness to which we should give prayerful consideration.[4]

The Bible also uses a variety of masculine metaphors for God. Some of these terms came from political or pastoral life, such as *king, judge, lord,* and *shepherd.* Other masculine metaphors came from family life and include *redeemer, brother, kinsman,* and *father.*

In Psalm 103:13, we are told, "As a father has compassion for his children, so the Lord has compassion for those who fear him." Jesus told us, "Pray then in this way: Our Father in heaven. . ." (Matthew 6:9). And in Romans 8:15-16 we are told that the Spirit of God empowers us to address God as "Abba," which may be properly translated "papa" or "daddy," an even more intimate and endearing term for father.

Clearly the metaphor "Father" is a prominent way to speak of God in the Bible, particularly in the New Testament. For me, it is a powerful and helpful way. The term *father* is one that will always be strong in my prayer, thought, and devotion. However, I honor the mysterious majesty of God if I do not make it the only metaphor or absolutize it over against all others.

Without pretending to be exhaustive or complete, in this brief discussion I have listed at least twenty biblical metaphors for God. Each one opens up new vistas of understanding and prayer for me.

However, this information may not be as comforting to others. Once, when I presented this material, a man responded, "This doesn't help me—dozens of pictures of God with little focus. It feels confusing and frustrating."

As we discussed how to put these many metaphors for God together, we found that some of them seem to be contradictory or opposite, or at least greatly different. We listed some of those: God as father and mother; as light and as hidden one; as lover and judge; as wrathful and tender. And there were many more. This led us to explore the concept of paradox—two seemingly contradictory thoughts, both true, but true only in relationship and tension with each other. Openly exploring all these metaphors, facing the differences and nuances, considering the paradoxes gave us fresh insights into the nature of God. We had become theologians! One man suggested, "Perhaps these images can be used as an orchestra to share with the world the loving music of God."

Part of my male faith journey, then, involves two recognitions: (a) the variety of gifts (including gifts for ministry) that God has given to persons, both women and men; (b) the multidimensional God I serve as revealed in the metaphors in the Bible. In both of these, I give up something that was once considered a male monopoly. In both of these, when I do, I grow, and others benefit as well.

Many Roads to Spiritual Growth

We begin with our basic understanding of and relationship with Jesus. We go on to a more inclusive vision. But then a basic question needs to be faced: How do we men grow spiritually? How can we experience closeness to God?

When I ask men when it is that they feel closest to God, I hear stories like these:

a. Some of the quickest responses had an outdoors theme. "I took the ski lift to the top on a clear morning after a fresh snow. I looked out at a world so pure and beautiful. And I thought, 'Wow, this is how it must have appeared to God, shortly after creation!'" "We rose early to go fishing and were just putting our boat in the water as the sun rose over the lake. The morning sounds, the ever-changing colors—what a God, what a world!" "My son and I climbed one of Colorado's 'fourteeners' (a fourteen-thousand-foot-high mountain) together. We climbed hard, took a few risks, helped each other. The view was magnificent—we felt so tiny in the vastness of it all. We couldn't stay as long as we wanted, because early afternoon lightning storms were threatening. And so we quickly descended to be away from that awesome and frightening power. It claimed all our strength and energy to do it, and yet we never felt closer to God—nor did my son and I ever feel closer to each other."

b. Others answer with athletic experiences. "I am a distance runner. There are two experiences in running that thrill me every time. For one, when my 'second wind' comes. One moment I am gasping for breath; the next moment, I have all the air I need to finish my run. The other is what people have called the 'runner's high.' At times there are moments of exhilaration that I can barely explain and that come at no other time. I feel so light, so good, so happy as I run. Every time it happens, I think of the verse, 'but those who wait for the Lord shall renew their strength, they shall mount up with wings like eagles, they shall run and not be weary, they shall walk and not faint' (Isaiah 40:31)."

"I love basketball and play pickup games whenever I can. Once in a great while, a team gets into 'the zone.' We pass without looking, anticipate, work, and come together better than we could imagine. It's poetry in motion! It's so much fun when it happens that you play again and again, looking for those rare moments. I had never thought of that as a spiritual moment until one day I read 1 Corinthians 12, 'If one member suffers, all suffer together . . . if one member is honored, all rejoice together. . . . Now you are the body of Christ and individually members of it.' That verse made me aware of God's presence in a group of us, working within us and beyond us."

c. Others respond in a different "hands-on" way. "I went to a work camp for Habitat for Humanity. We worked from sunup to dark to build a bunch of homes for homeless people. Those selected to live in the homes pitched in and worked hard—sweat equity they call it. At that camp they talked about 'the theology of the hammer.' That's how I feel. I express my faith through the things I can do for others with my hands—when there's a work day at my church, or a cry for help to fix up the yard of some elderly persons, I am there. The next year after the Habitat camp, I heard about my denomination's disaster response team. I volunteered and spent a week helping overwhelmed people haul out the mud and get things back in order after a flood. After a day of hard work for others, I look at myself in the mirror and I feel good inside. At such a time, I sense God is near."

d. A number of men individually told me something like this: "I felt God's presence when our baby was born. I was there in the delivery room, nervous and frightened for both my wife's and the baby's life. Then, after what seemed an eternity, there the baby was! They put her in my arms and I felt a fullness within I'd never known. At the same moment, the thought crossed my mind how much it would hurt ever to lose her. My wife and I now had someone else to live for. I was flooded with feelings of love—for my wife with whom I shared so much, for the baby whom I loved unconditionally from the moment of her birth. My heart was in my throat as I realized God had allowed us to share in this act of creation."

e. A few told me that they sensed God's presence in a person they really admired, someone who embodied what they wanted to be. Or they experienced God's presence in a group of people who made God's love real to them. Some told of going through a tragedy—a death in the family, the discovery they had a serious illness, the loss of a well-loved job—and being amazed at the creative love and support of people who saw them through. In that experience, they believed that God had loved them through those people.

f. Men spoke of experiencing God in beauty and in worship, sometimes at the same time. Singing inspired music, whether classical or contemporary, touched some men's souls. Participating in a drama made sacred truth all the more real. Other men spoke of the honor and privilege of assisting in worship, serving communion, ushering, or greeting and welcoming people. Some of these men added that somehow they worship better if they have one of these tasks to do. One should do something for God, they feel, and worship feels more connected when they are asked to do tasks that carry worship forward.

g. Some others told of feeling close to God in stillness or aloneness. One man loves the quiet of his home late at night. He likes to look in on his sleeping children, breathing his prayers for each, then sitting, reflecting, and giving thanks for those whom he loves. Another loves sitting on the porch of his summer home, enjoying the almost deserted lake, just reading and being. Those retreats when God is in the silence restore him for the hectic life he must live the rest of the year.

I'm sure many other answers could be given, but these are what I have heard as I have queried men about their spiritual lives. In some circumstances, men did not know they were talking about their spiritual lives and eventually discovered they were. All of the avenues of spirituality they described are available to women also, of course. And yet this list may describe some places of focus for men's spirituality.

Those in the a section described a nature-creation-ecological spirituality, one nurtured in the outdoors. Those in b described that close connection between body and spirit, how good care of the body feeds oneself spiritually, and how team sports can be an image of the spirit working in the body of Christ. The men in c gained the recognition that "just as you did it" to the least of Christ's brothers and sisters, you did it to him (Matthew 25:31-46), and in that, there is great spiritual joy. In d men were in touch with the spiritual awe of birth, parenting, and co-creation. Those in e found that God's presence and love were mediated by a person or group. Those in f have discovered how to worship the Lord in the beauty of holiness. In g we heard the testimony of those who resonate with the Scripture verse, "Be still, and know that I am

God!" (Psalm 46:10). Such men might want to cultivate more disciplined practices of meditation and prayer such as were described in chapter 3.

Any or all of these ways (or other ways) allow us to know God's presence and experience the life of the spirit. Anything that fits us is pleasing to God. We do not need to conform to someone else's idea of spirituality. One version of Romans 12:2 tells us, "Don't let the world around you squeeze you into its own mold, but let God remold your minds from within."[5] That's true even for our spiritual lives.

A Faith of Head, Heart, and Hand

Let's come at spiritual growth from a slightly different perspective. For all of us, our faith walk involves our *head* (thinking, reasoning), *heart* (feeling), and *hand* (doing). A life of commitment will include all three. However, it is quite all right that one of them be our dominant way in relating to our God.

For some of us, *thinking with our head* will be our predominant way of relating to God. We may use our minds to come to a reasonable faith or to arrive at our best understanding of the purpose of our lives. We may be fascinated by the puzzling moral dilemmas—both personal ones and issues facing our society—and explore ways to make decisions with integrity about such problems. We may hold to our course because we have thought, investigated, reasoned, and concluded. We have loved God with our minds.

I wish that we made more room for a faith of the head in the area of doubting, questioning, and searching. Far from denying faith, these may be ways of deepening faith. The Bible makes clear that God loves the doubters and searchers as well as those to whom faith comes more easily. It can be such a relief to be able to talk out loud about the questions that nag deep within and trouble us. For some of those, we must eventually come to a point where we live with the questions. I hope for men's groups, men's friendships, and churches that are open to this exercise of the mind.

Faith of the mind is desperately needed when we come to the task of sorting out the beliefs, practices, and issues of central importance. It is so easy for a group of Christian people to get tunnel vision on a single issue, to become convinced that one's stand on a single issue is *the* measure of faithfulness to God. We need persons with a thoughtful faith who will ask, "Is this the central issue of our times? Is there only one side on it, or are there several sides to this issue?" Such thoughtful Christians may save the church from tragic clashes and divisions.

For others of us, *feeling with our heart* will be our most basic way of relating to God. A huge gathering of Christian men may fill us with excitement. The beauty of a song or the winsomeness of a children's pageant or the sentiment of a hymn or the power of a dynamic speaker may move us to tears of joy. Humor and pranks among men may call forth laughter from deep within. Moments of prayer may fill us with ecstasy. St. Irenaeus once wrote, "Joy is the most unmistakable sign of the presence of God." For those of us who relate through the heart, not only joy but all emotions may be the evidence of God's presence and the way to experience that presence.

Others of us may relate to God through the *actions of our hands*. We are the pragmatic ones, the "can do" people. If we have a favorite hymn, it is "Christian, rise and *act* thy creed. Let thy prayer be in thy *deed*."[6] We connect to the men in paragraph (c) in the preceding section. In truth, we are a bit impatient when there are too few opportunities to relate to God through the service of our hands. The things we have built for God are a source of satisfaction through the years. The persons with whom we built something are folks who share a special bond.

Many churches make provision for the faith of the heart but don't provide much for faith of the head and hand. These may be male needs and male gifts. Men with these avenues of living out their faith should be honored. Churches should find more ways to participate in the faith walk of such men.

A Wide Choice of Heroes in the Faith

One of the gifts our Bible gives us is a wide variety of men who lived out their faith in God. There is great freedom in reflecting on this variety. In the Bible we find

wild men like Samson and John the Baptist;

a rough shepherd and dresser of sycamore trees—Amos;

persons who loved book learning and acquired wisdom, such as Solomon and Paul;

builders like Nehemiah;

skilled craftsmen such as Bezalel (Never heard of him? Look him up in Exodus 37-38);

adventurous warriors, such as Jonathan;

artists, poets, and songwriters, such as David;

questioners, searchers, those who looked for the deeper truth, such as Job and Habakkuk;

long-winded talkers, such as Paul;

quiet listeners and encouragers, such as Barnabas and Andrew;

impulsive folks like Peter and hesitant men like Moses;

melancholy, lonely men such as Jeremiah;

many men who were doers, not talkers, and men comfortable with the language of love, such as John the disciple.

In this list are rugged outdoorsmen and quiet indoor scholars. There are extroverts and introverts. There are those who never learned to read and lifelong scholars. There are married men, single men, men who had tragedy in their marriages (such as Hosea), and men who gave up hope of family because of God's call to them (such as Jeremiah). There are persons who are very close to God, and those who say they mostly wait for God without certainty of God's presence. There are persons with a vigorous, inspiring faith and vision, and those who keep on serving though they never see the promised land and struggle with doubt and searching.

As I consider the wide variety of men who loved and served God—men whom God loved and used in God's service—I see that there is hope for me. God must have a place for me with my gifts, interests, history, and temperament. This list again confirms that I do not need to conform to someone else's idea of what a Christian man should look like. I listen for God's quiet voice within telling me what to do with what I am for God.

I am told that the great medieval Jewish philosopher Maimonides once said, "On Judgment day, the Almighty will not ask me, 'Why were you not Moses?' Rather the Almighty will ask me, 'Why were you not Maimonides?'" In living with that question—how do I become the unique person that God intends me to be?—I find freedom, challenge, and joy.

A Male Style of Conversion

Some years ago, I read a quotation that helped me understand something that I had not previously understood—women's liberation. Two very able authors, Carol Christ and Marilyn Collins, explained it this way:

> Women's liberation is a *conversion experience*. For many women (and men) their conversion to the women's movement will be one of the two or three radical changes in their lives. A woman experiences vague apprehensions, . . . uneasiness. She feels she is odd because she is not always happy with the roles expected of her in society. . . . Suddenly it becomes clear. There is nothing wrong with her. The problem is that "women's role" does not fit women. The experience is sweet. "Liberation" is no longer a word; it becomes a deep penetrating sense of her potential. . . .
>
> [This] conversion . . . is structurally similar to conversion to a new religious consciousness. In this sense, women's liberation itself partakes of the numinous. Like other conversion experiences it is frightening as well as liberating. Social structures and institutions which had defined social reality are experienced as arbitrary and alienating. The center of reality changes.[7]

These authors suggest that a woman who finds her dignity and power within a movement experiences a kind of conversion. That makes sense to me. And I believe that there is a similar conversion available for men.

After all, there is nothing in the Bible that says we are limited to one conversion. As a matter of fact, the late theologian Nels Ferré (one of my mentors in the faith) used to say that he was converted three times: first to Christ as Lord and Savior, then to God as truth, and then to God as unconditional agape love. He spent the rest of his life writing about and living out those conversions.

And so conversions in a male mode may begin with a feeling of being drawn to a magnetic group of caring men, or perhaps to an entire church of caring people—a conversion to *Christ's people*. The next conversion may be to the one who is our Savior and Lord, our Pioneer and Friend—a conversion to *Christ's person*. The next conversion may be to making some big changes in one's life and doing some constructive things in the world. This may involve overcoming a habit or addiction that enslaves—a conversion to *Christ's purpose*.

Then one more conversion beckons to men—to claim what the Bible calls "the glorious liberty of the children of God" (Romans 8:21 RSV). By the grace of God as a man, I find my free fit in the world. I sense an inner liberty to be the man God calls me to be. I am allowed to be unembarrassed, indeed joyful, that this is not the clone or identical copy of any other men, not even those I admire most. When I claim that discovery, it leads me deeper into a loving relationship with God our source. Then I may indeed say that to experience my freedom under God as a Christian male is indeed a conversion experience. We might call it a conversion to *Christ's power.*

Invitations

Here are some areas of growth, discovery, or commitment you may want to explore:

__ Make a list of the people whose Christian life you admire. Talk to them about that and ask them to tell you about their joys and struggles as Christians.

_ Look up in the Bible the stories of some of the men
   mentioned and read about their faith journeys.

_ Write down a list of visions, dreams, hopes you have for
   yourself and those you hold dear. Beside each, write
   what first step you can take toward realizing those
   dreams.

_ Get to know a woman minister. Ask her about her call to
   ministry, about her joys and struggles in ministry.

_ Write your own:

_____

_____

Questions for Conversation and Group Discussion

1. How do you feel about your relationship to Jesus as
   Lord, Savior, Pioneer, and Friend? Are there other terms
   you would add to describe a full relationship with Jesus?

2. Try to make a list of at least twenty metaphors for God,
   either those provided in this chapter or others from the
   Bible. Which of these are most familiar and comfortable
   for you? Which of these do you have to stretch to accept?
   Which ones are nearly impossible for you to accept?
   Which ones seem paradoxical? Does this exercise
   stimulate your knowledge of God and relationship with
   God? If so, in what ways?

3. The author mentions some gifts he would like to use in
   the church that are usually thought of as women's gifts.
   Do you have some of those gifts as well? What has been
   your experience in offering them? What other gifts
   would you like to be free to offer? What gifts of women
   are not welcome in your church (you may want to ask
   women to help you answer that)?

4. Who are your favorite Bible characters? What do you
   admire most about them?

5. In the section "Many Roads to Spiritual Growth" the
   author lists several male experiences that open the way
   to spiritual growth. Which of those have you
   experienced? Which of those would you like to try? What
   others have you experienced?

6. What is your most basic way of relating to God—through head or heart or hands?

7. The author speaks of conversion to Christ's people, to Christ's person, to Christ's purpose, and to Christ's power. Which of those conversions have you experienced? Are you open to others of those conversions? What directions might these take?

Resources

Barclay, William. *The Letter to the Hebrews.* Edinburgh, Scotland: St. Andrew Press, 1955.

Christ, Carol, and Marilyn Collins. "Shattering the Idols of Men: Theology from the Perspective of Women's Experience." *Reflections* (Yale Divinity School, New Haven, Conn.) 69 (May 1972).

Key, William J., and Robert Johnson-Smith II, eds. *From One Brother to Another.* Valley Forge, Pa.: Judson Press, 1996.

Mollenkott, Virginia Ramey. *Women, Men, and the Bible.* Nashville: Abingdon Press, 1977.

Olson, Richard P. *Changing Male Roles in Today's World: A Christian Perspective for Men—and Women Who Care about Them.* Valley Forge, Pa.: Judson Press, 1982.

Sheldon, Charles. *In His Steps.* New York: Grosset and Dunlap, 1935.

Tolbert, Mary Ann. "The Bible and Sexist Language." In *Language about God in Liturgy and Scripture: A Study Guide.* Philadelphia: Geneva Press, 1980.

Weber, Stu. *Tender Warrior: God's Intention for a Man.* Sisters, Oreg.: Multnomah Books, Questar, 1993.

Notes

1. Charles Sheldon, *In His Steps* (New York: Grosset and Dunlap, 1935).

2. William Barclay, *The Letter to the Hebrews* (Edinburgh, Scotland: St. Andrew Press, 1955), 26.

3. Stu Weber, *Tender Warrior: God's Intention for a Man* (Sisters, Oreg.: Multnomah Books, Questar, 1993), 24.

4. Virginia Ramey Mollenkott, *Women, Men, and the Bible* (Nashville: Abingdon Press, 1977), 58.

5. J. B. Phillips, *The New Testament in Modern English* (New York: Macmillan, 1958).

6. The hymn "Christian, Rise and Act Thy Creed," written by F. A. Rollo Russell (1849–1914), is found in many hymnals.

7. Carol Christ and Marilyn Collins, "Shattering the Idols of Men: Theology from the Perspective of Women's Experience," *Reflections* (Yale Divinity School, New Haven, Conn.) 69 (May 1972); italics added.

8

Callings

He loved the peace and quiet that he finally experienced in his middle years. The earlier part of his life had been anything but that. He had been in danger for his life at birth, and only the courage and heroism of his mother and sister had saved him. Then there was the excitement of growing up as a privileged member of the royal court.

But then came the nagging questions—was he privileged Egyptian or was he Israelite? The answer came frighteningly one day when he saw an Egyptian taskmaster beating one of his Israelite kinfolk. Anger and patriotism overwhelmed him. In his rage, he killed the Egyptian and buried him in the sand. Too soon this secret crime was revealed.

Then came his desperate flight from the authorities into an unknown wilderness. In time, it had all worked out. He had found work as a herdsman and married the boss's daughter, who in turn gave him a son. A good family, good honest work—good *quiet* work—what more could a man want? He was glad to be away from all the turmoil.

But this peace and quiet was not to last. One day while tending the flocks, he saw a sight that stirred his curiosity: a bush that burned but was not consumed. When he drew close, the voice of God spoke to him out of that bush. God spoke of divine concern for Moses' people: "I have observed the misery of my people who are in Egypt; I have heard their cry on account of their taskmasters. Indeed, I know their sufferings, and I have come down to deliver them . . ." (Exodus 3:7-8). That sounded good, but the next words did not! The Lord continued, "So come, I will send *you* to Pharaoh to bring my people . . . out of Egypt" (v. 10; italics added). Walter Brueggemann, scholar of the Hebrew Scriptures, writes, ". . . the exodus has suddenly become a human enterprise. It is Moses (not God) who will meet with Pharaoh. It is Moses (not God) who will 'bring out' . . . 'my people.'"[1] Moses fearfully shrank back from this call. He did not want to face the dreaded authorities that earlier in his life he had fled! And so he offered five points of resistance concerning this new calling. Each of these objections looked at a past reality. Each time God responded by moving Moses into a new future.

Here are Moses's objections and God's responses:

1. I'm a genuine nobody. "Who am I that I should go . . . ?" God answers simply, "I will be with you" (Exodus 3:11, 12) and promises that as a sign, one day the people he leads will worship on the mountain where he stands at that moment.

2. "I don't know who you are; I don't know who is sending me." God both responds as the God of their ancestors and also reveals the name, "I AM WHO I AM." This name speaks of a divine presence that has power and fidelity. The name speaks of the power to create, to cause to be, to be there for Moses and the Israelites.[2]

3. My own people won't follow me: "suppose they do not believe me or listen to me" (Exodus 4:1). God's response is a question, "What is that in your hand?" Then God's response is an action. Moses casts down the rod in his hand. It becomes a serpent and changes to a rod when picked up.

4. I'm no speaker. "O my Lord, I have never been eloquent [not even after you called me] . . . but I am slow of speech and slow of tongue" (Exodus 4:10). God reminds him that it is God who gives speech to mortals. Further, "Now go, and I

will be with your mouth and teach you what you are to speak" (v. 12).

In spite of all this, Moses has one more objection.

5. "O my Lord, please send someone else." The Lord's anger is kindled against Moses. But as a concession to his weakness, God does provide his brother Aaron to go with him.

A fearful, resistant, unwilling man who felt inferior was called by God. The occasion for the call was the plight of a hurting, at-risk people. The task of the call was deliverance and liberation. And God prevailed! Reluctantly Moses headed back to Egypt to a task that was even more difficult and dangerous than he had feared. But God kept God's promises as well. Working through the man who responded to the call, God delivered an enslaved people.

Moses' story can propel us into the last topic of this book—our callings, yours and mine. This Bible account reminds us of a very basic message of the Bible, namely, that God calls us. God calls people to salvation. God calls us as communities to be people of God. Within those broader calls, God summons individuals to specific needs and tasks. Though we may no longer see burning bushes that are not consumed or hear an audible divine voice, still God speaks. God calls out of history and out of the present problems of our age. As with Moses, perhaps our memory of past injustices, our awareness of present problems, our sensitive conscience, our feeling "someone should do something about that," are the beginnings of our call. Then comes the quiet divine voice within, "You are that someone."

Like Moses, we come up with all sorts of excuses why we are *not* the ones for this calling, and like him we look at our past history to prove it. But if we are open and honest, God will prevail with us. As with Moses, God calls and guides us into a new future. Life will be richer, and people will be touched. Indeed, our lives will be filled with greater meaning, purpose, and mission as we respond to God's call.

What is it to which God is calling you or me? There are many possible callings, and I list a few possibilities in this chapter. However, these topics may be but a starting point for your discerning that to which God calls you.

The Calling to Embrace Our Dignity and Pride as Males

We begin with a basic call—to accept the dignity, the importance, the power of being a man. We hear so much anti-male rhetoric around, and so much blame, shame, and guilt are laid on men, that this may be hard to do. Like Moses before us, we may be tempted to cry out, "Who am I that I should answer this or any other call? If I believe what I read and hear, I am the problem, not part of the solution."

If we listen to our source, however, we receive a much calmer and more reassuring understanding of ourselves. The Bible makes clear that we are an important, basic part in God's creation:

> So God created humankind in his image,
>   in the image of God he created them,
>   male and female he created them.
> God blessed them. . . ."
>   —Genesis 1:27-28

In the image of God—both males and females! We are godlike in some important ways—perhaps in our abilities to create, to imagine, to dream, to relate, to worship, to pray. God's creation of us in God's image is wondrous indeed. God blesses persons' humanness. God also blesses our maleness as God blesses femaleness.

There are gifts and characteristics within our maleness that God can use. Tremendous power to achieve, to get things done, rests with groups of "can do" men. Further, good fun and fellowship are to be had by those who belong to such a group of men. Hurting boys, youths, and men can experience healing in the loving attention of a mature, caring man. Another man's friendship can banish loneliness. There are men to admire, and men who inspire us. We should not shrink from the possibility that each of us may be just such a man for someone.

A basic part of our call is to take pride in what God has ordained that we will be—men. We are to claim our dignity, knowing that it is more than OK, it is good to be what we are. God answers our resisting, shrinking "Who am I?" the same way God answered Moses' objection. We are told, "I will be with you."

Specifically, we may be called

to make a list of all the good things about being created male

to go to a humble man we admire and tell him what we admire in him

to share some of the joy and fun of being a man with a child or youth in our acquaintance

And there are many other opportunities.

The Calling to Us in Our Employment

Our call continues at our place of employment. Most of us men love to work at something we enjoy, something we're good at. Our occupation is an opportunity to live out part of our vocation.

Theologian Elton Trueblood once pointed out how employment can express our Christian calling. He said that three things should be true: (1) the work contributes to a good, a just, or at least a defensible end or product; (2) the relationships between people at work are conducted in a caring, helpful, and respectful manner; and (3) one's nonemployment time is used for other aspects of one's calling.[3]

However, many forces in the workplace these days make it increasingly difficult to live out such a calling at work. Employment is changing rapidly. Many persons once spent their entire career with one employer. Now it is estimated that persons will have—on the average—eight different careers, and many more employers than that. It's difficult to feel a part of things with such rapid change.

Further, employers are getting "leaner and meaner" in order to compete more effectively. One may do one's work well, only to be caught in an impersonal "downsizing." These repeated cutbacks threaten trust among co-workers. You don't want to reveal weaknesses that may be held against you, or get too close to the person with whom you may compete for one of the few remaining jobs. Fierce wars of competition are waged among industries but also among co-workers.

This downsizing occurs on every level of employment and responsibility. Men who have achieved a place of recognized leadership in one firm may have a long, difficult search to find a comparable position if they are dismissed. Men identify, perhaps overidentify, with their employment. And so it may be extremely difficult to retain a sense of calling and dignity in those long one-, two- or three-year intervals when one is seeking a new position.

Those who keep working may no longer hold the expectation of a gradual increase in pay and responsibility. One may need to run hard just to stay even. A sense of security may feel even more tenuous for young adults, and especially for minority young adult men, trying to gain a foothold in the employment scene. They are the last hired and first fired.

The shortage of opportunities may also make it more difficult to select employment where one is proud of the employer, goals, and products. One may need to take whatever job one can find!

Another important part of the current work scene is the growing number of persons who opt for self-employment, perhaps developing some service they can deliver out of their homes. This employment may be more controllable, but it may also feel more lonely.

Men of all ages are also learning about the new gender mix in the workplace. Increasingly women are working at all levels of responsibility, in larger numbers, and in lifelong careers. In this new environment some of the rules, assumptions, and expectations are changing. Language and teasing that once went unchallenged may now be considered sexual harassment with serious implications for one's employment. Friendships, teamwork, romantic attraction, socializing—

all of these need to be considered in the light of gender justice and partnership in the workplace.

Where the workplace once felt comfortable, there may be considerable tension now. Uncertainty, frequent change, competition, a struggle to survive, the need to learn new rules—all these and more are part of the employment scene. This changed employment environment is a more difficult place to live out God's call than the one that existed when Elton Trueblood wrote of occupation as calling. And yet, now more than ever, men are needed to be God's persons in the workplace. God calls us in the midst of all these struggles. We are called

to give an honest day's work for a day's pay

to avoid emphasizing employment so much that we ignore marriage and family life as well as other opportunities to relate and serve

to live within our income (and save some) so that we can live more easily with the uncertainty of employment and the possibilities of unemployment

to overcome competitive fears and still build friendship and support with co-workers

to be available to help, guide, and encourage the beginner and the person struggling to make it

to be fair and just in our own competition for jobs and promotions, regardless of what others may do

to be positive, open, cooperative, and willing to learn how to relate with women colleagues

to look for those times to share an appropriate word of witness about our faith and values or an invitation to our men's group and church

to find our calling in enough places that we can stand the ravages of unemployment and retirement

to be supportive of other men going through unemployment and retirement

And there are undoubtedly more.

The Calling to Be Mentor and Volunteer

In his important book, *The Wonder of Boys,* Michael Gurian writes, "My basic vision of how to love a boy always returns to the insight that *three families—not one—raise a healthy boy to healthy manhood.*"[4] The first family is the boy's birth or adoptive parents and grandparents. The second family is the boy's "extended family," which includes blood relatives, adult friends, day-care providers, teachers, peers, and mentors. The third family is the culture and community in which the boy is raised—figures in the media, church groups, community, government, and other institutions.

Gurian maintains that when these three families do not coordinate efforts or build communal values together, or do not make childraising the primary purpose of culture, then the child feels unsafe and unloved. Then boys may feel it necessary to build their own peer-dominated culture, and the subgroups they form may well be antisocial. Only in a setting in which all three families work together will boys be raised to fulfill the four basic goals of responsible adult life, which Gurian lists as making a contribution to society; making a commitment to a mate; fulfilling responsibility for children; and continuing in spiritual growth.[5]

Gurian's vision is a prophetic call to caring Christian men: to make sure that every boy and girl has all three families, to be vital parts of all three families for the children in our communities. Gurian's vision draws us back urgently to the call to mentoring of which I spoke earlier. We use that term so much these days that we may fail to notice how many things it can mean. Basically it means sharing my presence; my hobbies and interests; my guidance and support in career discovery and development; my faith, values, and commitments—or maybe all of the above—with another person, usually younger than I.

This is the work of the second family in Gurian's scheme. And in this work we men need a nudge. Somehow we fail to realize what a powerful impact we can have and how tragic is the absence of mentoring. The result is that there is much greater demand for caring male mentors than can currently be met.

I heard an elementary school principal tell how much it means to at-risk children to have a caring adult friend come and eat lunch with that child for one hour a week. But she had a difficult time finding men for the male children.

I have heard single mothers lament the lack of a caring male presence in their sons' lives. They had applied to Big Brothers programs but had been told of a shortage so severe that there would be a wait of months or maybe even years before an adult man would be available for their sons.

I am told that many gang members in inner cities not only do not have an adult male mentor but have never known one. This need is coming into greater prominence. In 1997, a national conference on volunteerism, endorsed by all living American presidents, focused on the need to provide services and relate to the severely at-risk young people in our culture.

I hear of the struggle and near-despair for young adult males (perhaps high school dropouts, perhaps high school or college or military graduates) trying to get a start in finding a job, doing well, getting established in a career. This pain is especially strong in African American and Hispanic young adult males.

The good news is that there are strong, gentle, wise Christian males to meet each of these needs. The bad news is that they do not yet know they are called to this great opportunity. Nor do they recognize the gifts they have to give in such a relationship. Listen not only for your call to mentoring but for the specific child, youth, young adult, or program where you can start.

A parallel call is to be a volunteer in some area of need. When I was a young teenager, our church building burned down. With some paid employees and much volunteerism, we set about to build a new church. Every day that I could, all summer long, I helped. I didn't have many skills—often I hauled out the debris, swept up the sawdust, filled in trenches. But together we built a church. A few years later, my denomination was building a new camp and conference center. Again I volunteered for a summer. That time, I could do a little more—hauling cement, nailing on siding, putting on shingles. To this day these two experiences are among the most satisfying in my life.

Such stories could be repeated many times. A close friend tells me that the most enriching thing he has done in recent years was to participate in a Jimmy Carter Habitat for Humanity Work Week. The long hours of hard work, the camaraderie, and the joy of rehabilitating several homes for previously homeless people were more fulfilling than any vacation or conference in which he had participated for years! Or the volunteerism could involve not building something new but helping people recover from a disaster such as the recent flooding in Ohio and North Dakota.

God's call will match our gifts. Like Moses, we may not yet know what those gifts are. As with him, the gifts will be revealed in the doing. For some, the gift may include conceiving, organizing, and leading such projects. For others, it may be pitching in, following, sweating it out. In our own community, across our land, around the world, many projects await the willing hands and hearts of people who have responded to the call.

Perhaps the call to mentor and to volunteer will come together. Take the person you mentor on a volunteerism project. Work side by side. Teach him or her some new skills and work habits. Experience the joy, the sense of accomplishment together that comes from a job well done in the service of other human beings.

Specifically, we may be called

> to reach out to a child or youth known to us, perhaps in our church, perhaps in our neighborhood
>
> to investigate places where adult male presence is wanted and needed—in schools, Big Brothers programs, and more
>
> to create a mentoring program in our church
>
> to volunteer for one activity to which we feel drawn but which we have never done before

And there are many more opportunities.

The Calling to Us as Sexual Beings

There are other areas in which to live out our call. Having a graceful approach to sex is one such area.

Sam Keen notes, "Statisticians and psychologists have established that boys, once aroused to sex, think about it on the average of six times an hour on a slow day."[6] And for many of us males, our sex drive does not slow down much, for a long time afterward!

In this book, I have spoken of sex on several occasions because it is such a vital, vibrant part of who we are. Sex is a strong human urge. As Christians we understand that God created us—all of us. Therefore God created us with this urge, this drive, this passion; God also has a purpose and direction for it. Like every other gift from God, this one can be used for beautiful and constructive ends, or it can hurt, degrade, and destroy people. Our call is to discover how to exercise our sexuality constructively. Sexual passion and spiritual passion are closely related. Finding a positive direction and channel for our sexual energy has rich spiritual rewards.

As we begin that search, we note that males and females experience sex differently. Barbara Dafoe Whitehead recently wrote, "Despite changes in teenage sexual behavior, boys and girls continue to view love and sex relationships in different ways. Girls look for security, and boys seek adventure. Boys are after variety, and girls want intimacy. The classic formulation still seems to hold true: girls give sex in order to get love and boys give love in order to get sex."[7] Throughout our life, our search for sexual communion will be complicated—and enlivened—by the continuation of such differences.

We must also be aware that we live in a sick, satiated, and confused society where sexual matters are concerned. A recent study discovered that an average American teen watches 14,000 sexual encounters a year on television alone.

Such a permissive view in television and most other media has its effect. According to studies by the Guttmacher Institute, three-quarters of today's boys and one-half of today's girls have had intercourse by the time they graduate from high school. The average age for first intercourse is 16.6 for boys and 17.4 for girls. About 30 percent of teenagers did not use any birth control method at their first intercourse, and a much larger percentage did not use it consistently. The rate of teenage pregnancy in the United States is one of the highest in the world. AIDS and other sexually transmitted diseases are spreading fastest among teens and young adults regardless of sexual orientation.

So far I have described what is presumed to be consensual sex. Yet another grim part of the picture is coerced sex. The dimensions of the problem of date rape are now being acknowledged. One study found that 25 percent of men had tried to have intercourse with a woman against her wishes. Yet another study concluded that 25 percent of women had experienced first intercourse because of force or a sense of obligation.[9] Victims of such behavior report that the pain remains for years afterward. Add to these statistics the tragic discovery that at least one in four girls and one in seven boys are sexually molested, usually by someone they know. On top of that we read about the recurring scandals of sexual harassment in the military services. Clearly something has gone tragically wrong with the expression of sexuality in our society.

And that is our calling: to claim a vision of the purpose of sex and of ways to guide and channel this awesome power, first for ourselves, and then for those whom we influence. In search of this understanding, Michael Gurian looks wistfully at some tribal cultures that do a much better job in this area.

In these societies boys are taught that sex is sex, a natural biological act, not shameful in the least, in fact sacred; boys are taught that love, ardor, Eros is a mysterious emotional relationship with others, nerve-wracking but ultimately rewarding; boys are taught that commitment is a socially mandated role that allows for the male to have sex, experience love, care for his wife, children, and serve the great cycle of life.[10]

Such resources, and more, are available within our Christian faith. We are called

to acknowledge God's good gift of sex and to feel free to celebrate it and discuss it often with our children. Our discussions will include our moral values and commitments.

to act and teach our children to act responsibly. That is to say that sexual expression should be mutual, and it should match the commitment of two people to each other. A Christian understanding of sex needs a balance of healthy appreciation and disciplined obedience. The Bible offers a number of "Thou shalt not's" as an expression of this balance.

to recognize that although intercourse should be postponed until young people are more mature, they are not denied sexual expression. As Jack Balswick points out, "Authentic sexuality is much more than intercourse; it involves touch to communicate tenderness, affection, solace, understanding, desire, warmth, comfort, and excitement."[11] Learning, enjoying, experimenting with those sexual gifts, can be constructive and can contribute to strengths in loving throughout a lifetime.

to discover that the way to be a great lover is to make an enduring commitment and then to find new and creative ways to love that same person for the rest of one's life.

None of the above comments will remove all of the mystery we enjoy or the problems we may experience from our persistent sex drive. But they do lead us in the direction of responding to the call God gave us when God created us as sexual beings.

The Calling to Support Women

Further, in seeking a better way for us men to live, we are called to want a better life for women as well. We need not feel bad, guilty, or inferior because we are different from women in many ways. Male emotions, friendships, parenting methods, communication styles, sexuality, and spirituality may be quite different from that of females. Neither style is right, and neither is wrong. Neither is "good," and neither is "bad." The two styles are simply different from each other. We can be at peace about that.

We have mentioned several places in our culture where experiences for us males are harsh. Even so, we are called to recognize and confront the places in our culture where females have harsh experiences. Junior high girls should not have to face pressing decisions about sex, drugs, and alcohol. Young women should not be pressured or subjected to date rape. Women should not feel unsafe or be the object of violence—not on the street, not in their homes. When employed, women have a right to equal pay for equal work and access to all the opportunities for growth and advancement in the workplace that men have. In the church, women's responses to God's call should be affirmed, encouraged, celebrated, and accepted.

Any gain in my life as a man will be hollow if it is not accompanied by a corresponding gain for the women I care about. I seek a greater vision, self-understanding, and inner freedom for us men. I also desire a better world for my wife, daughters, granddaughters, biological sister, sisters in Christ, sisters in humanity.

Let us consider a call

to resist gender stereotypes, sexist jokes, or ganging up as one gender against another at work

to welcome, affirm, and accept women colleagues

if one is married, to discuss with one's wife what in the marriage needs to be addressed with regard to mutual equality and respect

if one is a parent, to have equally high aspirations and commitments for children of both genders, and equally frank discussions about the pains, dangers, and injustices in their world

at church, to take the leadership in helping to expand notions about fitting leadership roles for women and for men

And there are certainly more.

The Call to Explore Matters of Age and Race

In an excellent anthology about men, editor Francis Baumli writes that he has drawn together a comprehensive description of the male experience. But he adds this note:

> I must qualify this statement. Despite my best efforts, I was unable to get sufficient articles of high quality to have sections on *aging* and on *men of color.* Perhaps my lack of success in these areas points to current limitations in the men's liberation movement. Perhaps we do not have the desire, or the courage, to come to grips with the process of aging in a personal, honest way. And perhaps the boundaries—both explicit and subtle—that separate the races in our culture have not been examined sufficiently by the men's movement.[12]

In the current men's movements, little attention is given to aging and elderly men. That is no surprise to me. We live in a society that exalts youthfulness; a thin, lithe figure; a wrinkle-free face; hair with no gray. We honor physical strength and agility.

Men participate in such thinking and emphasize some aspects of it even more. If a man is to be physically strong, competitive, and athletic, then aging is bad news indeed. If the youthful look is needed to be appealing to women, men may go to great extremes to hide every sign of aging. It's a sad day for a man when he realizes that his age shows too much for him to compete for a woman's smile and attention.

Further, men often identify manliness with being productive. Retiring from the workforce is not something that many men do gracefully. If we are not employed, if we are not producing something, we sense we have lost something masculine.

I recently experienced a striking contrast to this cultural attitude. As a man in his sixties, I wistfully recall my recent stay for a few months in Southeast Asia. There age is much more highly respected, honored, revered. Young people called me "uncle" or "father" or "grandpa" with affection and high regard. My students willingly spent time with me, sharing information, often asking for my perceived wisdom on some topic. Even as a novice in their culture, I felt good being an older man there!

I conclude that we are called to learn some things and change some things in our attitudes about aging. A new comfort, a new inclusiveness is needed among Christian men. Indeed we will be wise if we make men's groups inter-generational and take time to listen to each generation. Specifically, we may be called

to come to grips with the facts of our own aging process

to acknowledge our age, act our age, accept our age

to befriend and listen with respect to older men in our family and church and among our acquaintances

to turn to older men and women for "living history" of our community and our church, learning their wisdom and concerns for the future

to do what is necessary—such as providing transportation—to be sure that older men are included in our groups

Baumli also said he could not find sufficient material about men of color. He wrote before the Million Man March, and perhaps his finding helps to explain why such a move-ment needed to come into being—none of the other move-ments sufficiently included men of color or listened well enough to their concerns.

In a multicultural world, in a church where we are called to break all barriers down, men are called to reach out to each other across racial lines. This will most likely happen if several elements come together. We will need genuinely to want reconciliation of the races and the privilege of knowing some persons we have not previously known. We will need to be willing to listen, to respect, and to work on each other's concerns. Opinions on justice issues, on which there may be legitimate differences, may need to be aired. It may be that these justice issues will require action and attention. Per-sons will need to be willing to hear another's experience and perhaps to change.

Perhaps the reconciliation will proceed if we find a way to work side by side. I am aware of two churches—one predominantly Euro-American and one predominantly African American—that teamed together to build a Habitat for Humanity home. Though the task was demanding and exhausting, the joint effort was a community-building activity indeed. The reconciliation will be enhanced by our listening to each other's testimonies about our faith pilgrimages and by our worshipping together, learning from each other new dimensions of worship.

We need each other—the other's strength, wisdom, energy, and help on tasks too big for one racial group alone. Our communities need the modeling of men who reach out to each other to reconcile in faith, in justice, in service, and in relationship building. Specifically, we may be called

to meet, interview, get to know at least one person of a race or culture different from our own

to invite an international student into our home

to initiate joint meetings, worship experiences, or projects with men from a church of a racial or cultural group different from our own

Other Callings

We are called to grow, to seek to be mature men. This calling involves a thoughtfulness, a willingness to learn, an awareness of the lessons of history. It calls for a thoughtful, reasoned use of Scripture, not a slavish, literalistic biblicism. It includes willingness (maybe even eagerness) to dialogue with persons whose viewpoints are quite different from our own. The goal of such dialogue will not be to convince the other but to expand one's world by hearing another view.

Men who respond to such a calling may grow to be the statesmen, the persons of vision, understanding, and inclusiveness needed in such a time as this. Such men are peacemakers, whom Jesus blessed and whom the world so desperately needs.

We are called to care for the earth. Many of us as small boys felt most at home in the outdoors. Only reluctantly did we answer that evening call to come inside for food and bed. We enjoyed our camp-outs as Scouts, our church camps, often in some beautiful natural place in God's creation. As men we treasure our annual fishing or hunting trips, our hikes and mountain-climbing expeditions, our skiing adventures. God restores us in the outdoors.

But those places of renewal in nature are shrinking and becoming more crowded. Our planet's fragile ecology is threatened. And so we are called not only to enjoy God's beautiful earth but to care for it. We are to lobby for it, recycle and preserve its nonrenewable resources, work to limit its population growth, vote for and pay for parks and natural recreation areas. Future generations' spiritual and physical welfare depends on our commitment to this earth.

And each of us will recognize other callings—places to care, places to serve, places to be God's man.

Conclusion

On these pages we have listened to the voices of many men on topics that are important to us. We have discovered more about why we are the way we are and received glimpses of who we can be. We have heard of problems that are caused by our negligence and have received calls to be part of the solution.

We may have concluded that we males are not as bad as sometimes described, and not as good as we could be. But that is not the end of the story. God's gracious call comes to each of us. When we respond, we are gradually transformed into God's caring, gentle men. We catch a vision of the fathers, sons, brothers, friends, co-workers, mentors, and volunteers we can be. Like Moses, we hear our God saying, "I am at work responding to the cries of a hurting world. Come join me," and we follow.

Invitations

In this chapter, the invitations are given at the end of each section. Go back, read them, and select those to which you wish to commit.

Questions for Conversation and Group Discussion

1. Where do you experience "put-downs" of males or find your dignity as a male challenged or undermined? How do you respond to those experiences? What steps can you take to lay hold of your dignity as a man?
2. When are the hardest times to live as a Christian at work? What opportunities have you taken to live as a Christian at work?
3. What are the opportunities for mentoring in your community? What most appeals to you as a place to start in this calling?
4. What most surprised you about the discussion of sex as a calling? What would you most like to see changed in the way our culture addresses sexuality? What can you do to give faithful expression to sex as a calling?
5. What injustices do the women you care about encounter? What avenues of being supportive are open to you?
6. Who are the persons of other generations from whom you have learned the most? What did you learn? Whom from other generations would you like to meet and interview?
7. What are the nearest and best opportunities you have for friendship across racial or cultural lines?
8. What do you treasure most about nature and the outdoors? What can you do to preserve the earth?

Resources

Balswick, Jack. *Men at the Crossroads: Beyond Traditional Roles and Modern Options.* Downers Grove, Ill.: InterVarsity Press, 1992.

Baumli, Francis, ed. *Men Freeing Men: Exploding the Myth of the Traditional Male.* Jersey City: New Atlantis Press, 1985.

Brueggemann, Walter. "The Book of Exodus." In *The New Interpreter's Bible,* vol. 1. Nashville: Abingdon Press, 1994.

Gurian, Michael. *The Wonder of Boys: What Parents, Mentors, and Educators Can Do to Shape Boys into Exceptional Men.* New York: Jeremy P. Tarcher/Putnam Book, 1996.

Keen, Sam. *Fire in the Belly: On Being a Man.* New York: Bantam Books, 1991.

Nelson, James B. *Embodiment.* Minneapolis: Augsburg Press, 1978.

Trueblood, Elton. *Your Other Vocation.* New York: Harper and Brothers, 1952.

Notes

1. Walter Brueggemann, "The Book of Exodus," in *The New Interpreter's Bible,* vol. 1 (Nashville: Abingdon Press, 1994), 713.

2. Ibid., 714.

3. Elton Trueblood, *Your Other Vocation* (New York: Harper and Brothers, 1952), 69.

4. Michael Gurian, *The Wonder of Boys: What Parents, Mentors, and Educators Can Do to Shape Boys into Exceptional Men* (New York: Jeremy P. Tarcher/Putnam Book, 1996), 58.

5. Ibid., 59.

6. Sam Keen, *Fire in the Belly: On Being a Man* (New York: Bantam Books, 1991), 72.

7. Barbara Dafoe Whitehead, cited in Gurian, *Wonder of Boys,* 225.

8. Gurian, *Wonder of Boys,* 222-23.

9. Jack Balswick, *Men at the Crossroads: Beyond Traditional Roles and Modern Options* (Downers Grove, Ill.: InterVarsity Press, 1992), 107.

10. Gurian, *Wonder of Boys,* 227.

11. Balswick, *Men at the Crossroads,* 118.

12. Francis Baumli, ed., *Men Freeing Men: Exploding the Myth of the Traditional Male* (Jersey City: New Atlantis Press, 1985), x.